MW00610396

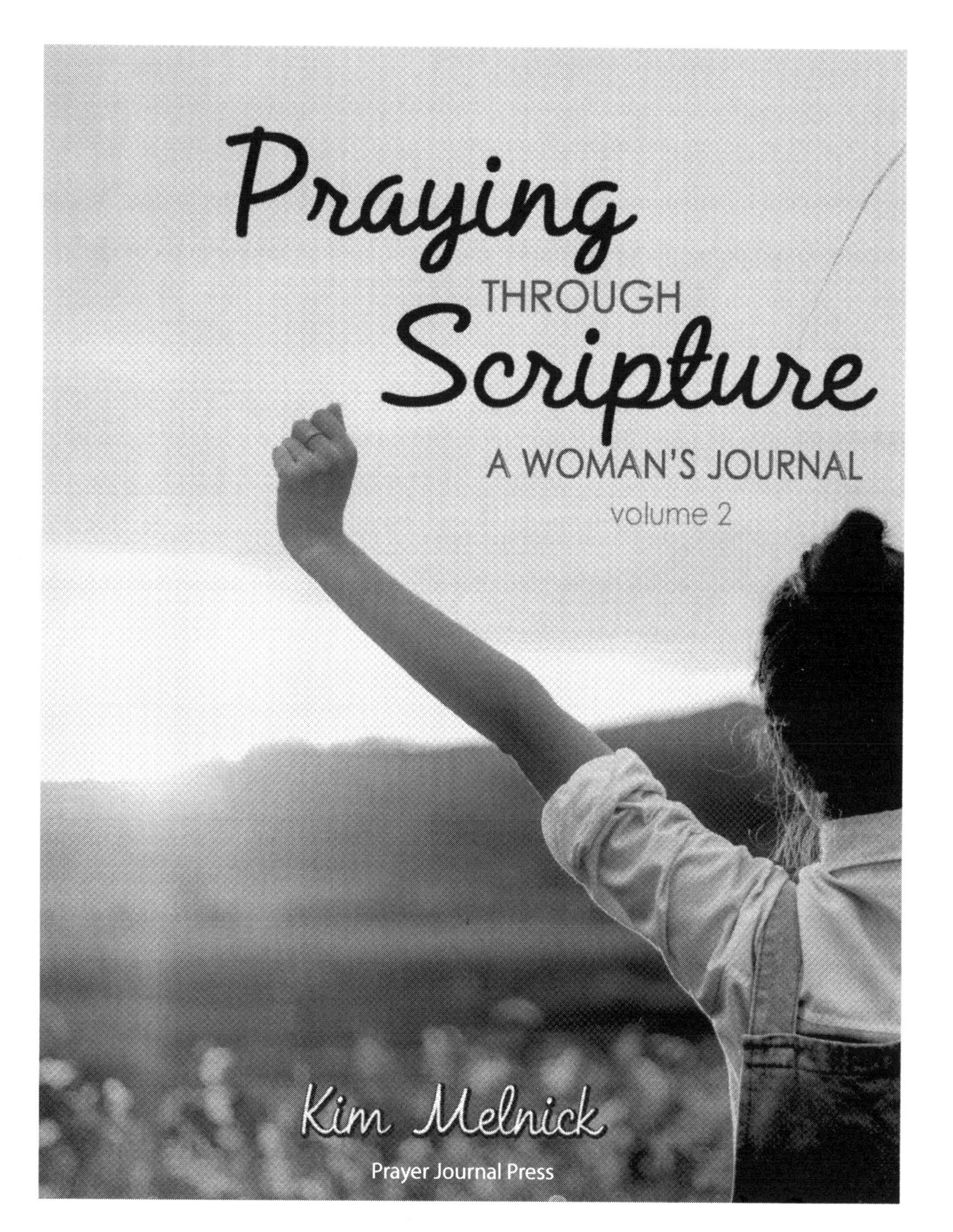
Praying
THROUGH
Scripture
A WOMAN'S JOURNAL
volume 2
Kim Melnick
Prayer Journal Press

Praying Through Scripture - A Woman's Journal - Volume 2

Prayer Journal Press
ISBN 978-0-9995857-2-6

Other titles available:
Praying Through Scripture - A Woman's Journal - Volume 1 (ISBN 978-0-9995857-1-9)
Praying Through Scripture - A Woman's Journal - King James Version (ISBN 978-0-9995857-3-3)
e-Book (PDF) versions available on our website

All inquiries should be sent through Contact page on our website, www.PrayWithScripture.com.

Cover design and layout by Jeff Melnick, High Impact Advertising LLC (www.hiashop.com)

Page design inspired by Amanda Melnick

Printed in the United States of America

2018 - First Edition

Foreword

Prayer Warrior Wannabe

I wrote this book for myself. Seriously. While that may seem a little strange, it's the truth.

I have loved Jesus for many years. I love His Word and I'm pretty faithful in reading or studying it everyday. I love to listen to sermons and be wowed by some mind-blowing connection between the Old and New Testaments that I had missed. I love when a familiar passage takes on new depth as I learn the true meaning of a word in the original Greek or Hebrew. In short, I LOVE learning about our amazing God through His Word.

But with prayer, I struggle. For years, I wanted to love prayer, to be that woman who rises early and often, who spends long and precious moments with the Lord in praise of Him and in supplication for others and for herself. However, I'm not that woman. When I pray early, my mind wanders to the demands of the day. When I pray late, my energy wanes and sleep overtakes me and often cannot find words to express what my heart longs to say.

Years ago, I learned the "secret of prayer" from a favorite pastor's sermon. He said to simply make GOD'S will YOUR wants. Then, ask for whatever you want! I loved this idea and sought ways to apply it to my prayer life. I began asking God, after a time of reading or studying, to show me how to use what I just learned about Him/His will to pray for myself and those around me.

This was helpful, but I still felt distracted in my prayer time. On top of that, there were people and situations that I desired to pray for on a regular basis, but still did not do so. That's where the writing of this book begins....

I began collecting verses and organizing them by categories of prayer - by topics that I wanted to pray for regularly. Initially, there were verses scribbled on various pieces of notebook paper and in prayer journals. Eventually, they were organized. As I began to use them in my personal prayer time, I learned that these categories really did help my focus. And, by praying specific bible verses with each category, I no longer had to "find" the words to pray. God had already given them to me.

With much help from my husband and some design input from my 12 year old daughter, our first book (Volume 1) began to take shape. Instead of normal "proof-reading," the book was checked through "prayer-reading." For both Volume 1 and Volume 2, I've prayed through every verse and every page.

While I'm still a Prayer Warrior Wannabe, thanks to the grace of God and the contents of our Praying Through Scripture books, I've come a long way!

How to Use This Book

I'm sure there are countless ways to use this book, but here I will cover how I use it. Each "section" of the book is six pages long and I recommend using a section for one to two weeks.

Categories/Topics (Listed at the top of each column)
The first page of each section is designed to prepare your heart and mind to pray: Adoration, Confession and Thanksgiving. These are pretty self-explanatory and the verses given for Adoration and Thanksgiving make it easy to give praise and thanks to the Lord.

With Confession, there is also a verse to pray, reminding us of our sinful nature and of God's grace and mercy in forgiveness. When I'm reflecting on my own sin, I often examine my past day/week while reflecting on the fruits of the Spirit (love, joy, patience, kindness, goodness, faithfulness). This allows me to quickly identify sin in my life.

The remaining categories are listed below along with prompts on how I view this category….

Children - My own children/others I know or care about

Marriages - My marriage, married friends, marriages in my church, engaged couples, my own children whom I hope to see find a Godly spouse

Finances/Stewardship - My own/those around me, especially those who are struggling

The Church - The body of Christ where I worship and the Church worldwide

Nation/Leaders - Our President, Congress and other national/state/local leaders and citizens

Missionaries - Those who have left home to share the Gospel of Jesus full-time

The Lost - Family/Friends/Acquaintances whose lives have not been transformed by the Gospel of Jesus Christ

The Sick, Weary & Discouraged - General category for those burdened by various struggles

The Oppressed & Enslaved - General category that might include those who are suffering from persecution, addiction, or caught human trafficking

Wisdom - For myself and those who are in situations where a need for wisdom is apparent

Daily Walk - Myself and others who may be struggling with faithfulness, obedience, etc

Gratitude & Joy - Myself and others who need a reminder that we always have a reason for joy and gratitude

How to Use This Book

Bible Verses

I encourage you to read the verse a few times. Consider how you might pray this verse for the people or situations that come to mind with the prompt. In most instances, I actually pray the verse back to God. For example, if I'm praying Proverbs 5:16 for my husband, I might say, "Lord, help Jeff to shine your light today that others may see his good deeds and glorify you."

Journal Space

Some of you love to journal; others hate it. This space was intentionally left small for those who might be intimidated by large chunks of lined space. If you love to write out long prayers, go for it and know that there is full page of journaling at the end of each week's section if you run out of room. I personally love the idea of journaling more than the actual practice of journaling out long passages or prayers, so I use the space to make lists or bullet points. I would encourage you to write something, even if it's just a few words. It will help keep you focused, and you will have a resource to look back and see how God worked in various situations.

Weird Letters at the Bottom of the Page

Those weird letters at the bottom of the page are not typos. They are a tool to help you memorize Scripture. Each letter is the first letter of every word in the verses listed on the page. You can look at the letters and recall the words pretty easily. If you do this regularly, you will have memorized the verse. If you make this a practice as you pray, this book will help you memorize sixty verses as you pray.

Adoration

Great and marvelous are your deeds, Lord God Almighty. Just and true are your ways, King of the nations. Who will not fear you, Lord, and bring glory to your name? For you alone are holy. All nations will come and worship before you, for your righteous acts have been revealed.
Revelation 15:3b-4

Confession

Those whom I love I rebuke and discipline. So be earnest and repent. Here I am! I stand at the door and knock. If anyone hears my voice and opens the door, I will come in and eat with that person, and they with me.
Revelation 3:19-20

Thanksgiving

Every good and perfect gift is from above, coming down from the Father of the heavenly lights, who does not change like shifting shadows.
James 1:17

G A M A Y D, L G A. J A T A Y W, K O T N. W W N F Y, L, A B G T Y N? F Y A A H. A N W C A W B Y, F Y R A H B R. - Revelation 15:3b-4

T W I L I R A D. S B E A R. H I A! I S A T D A K. I A H M V A O T D, I W C I A E W T P, A T W M. - Revelation 3:19-20

E G A P G I F A, C D F T F O T H L, W D N C L S S. - James 1:17

Children

Behold, children are a gift of the Lord. The fruit of the womb is a reward. Like arrows in the hand of a warrior, so are the children of one's youth.
Psalm 127:3-4

Marriages

Two are better than one, because they have a good reward for their labor. For if they fall, one will lift up his companion. But woe to him who is alone when he falls, for he has no one to help him up.
Ecclesiastes 4:9-10

Finances & Stewardship

Choose a good reputation over great riches; being held in high esteem is better than silver or gold. The rich and poor have this in common: The Lord made them both.
Proverbs 22:1-2

B, C A A G O T L. T F O T W I A R. L A I T H O A W, S A T C O O Y. - Psalm 127:3-4

T A B T O, B T H A G R F T L. F I T F, O W L U H C. B W T H W I A W H F, F H H N O T H H U. - Ecclesiastes 4:9-10

C A G R O G R; B H I H E I B T S O G. T R A P H T I C: T L M T B. - Proverbs 22:1-2

The Church

God is spirit, and those who worship him must worship in spirit and truth.
John 4:24

Nations & Leaders

The king's heart is a stream of water in the hand of the Lord; he turns it wherever he will.
Proverbs 21:1

Missionaries

Preach the word of God. Be prepared, whether the time is favorable or not. Patiently correct, rebuke, and encourage your people with good teaching.
2 Timothy 4:2

G I S, A T W W H M W I S A T. - John 4:24

T K H I A S O W I T H O T L; H T I W H W. - Proverbs 21:1

P T W O G. B P, W T T I F O N. P C, R, A E Y P W G T. - 2 Timothy 4:2

The Lost

And I will give them one heart, and a new spirit I will put within them. I will remove the heart of stone from their flesh and give them a heart of flesh, that they may walk in my statutes and keep my rules and obey them. And they shall be my people, and I will be their God.
Ezekiel 11:19-20

The Sick, Weary & Discouraged

Fear not, for I am with you; be not dismayed, for I am your God; I will strengthen you, I will help you, I will uphold you with my righteous right hand.
Isaiah 41:10

The Oppressed & Enslaved

The Spirit of the Lord is upon me, because he has anointed me to proclaim good news to the poor. He has sent me to proclaim liberty to the captives and recovering of sight to the blind, to set at liberty those who are oppressed.
Luke 4:18

A I W G T O H, A A N S I W P W T. I W R T H O S F T F A G T A H O F,
T T M W I M S A K M R A O T. A T S B M P, A I W B T G. - Ezekiel 11:19-20

F N, F I A W Y; B N D, F I A Y G; I W S Y, I W H Y, I W U Y W M R R H. - Isaiah 41:10

T S O T L I U M, B H H A M T P G N T T P. H H S M T
P L T T C A R O S T T B, T S A L T W A O. - Luke 4:18

Wisdom

Don't be impressed with your own wisdom. Instead, fear the Lord and turn away from evil. Then you will have healing for your body and strength for your bones.
Proverbs 3:7-8

Daily Walk

Take delight in the Lord, and he will give you your heart's desires. Commit everything you do to the Lord. Trust him, and he will help you.
Psalm 7:4-5

Gratitude & Joy

I pray that God, the source of hope, will fill you completely with joy and peace because you trust in him. Then you will overflow with confident hope through the power of the Holy Spirit.
Romans 15:13

D B I W Y O W. I, F T L A T A F E. T Y W H H F Y B A S F Y B. - Proverbs 3:7-8

T D I T L, A H W G Y Y H D. C E Y D T T L. T H, A H W H Y. - Psalm 7:4-5

I P T G, T S O H, W F Y C W J A P B Y T I H. T Y W O W C H T T P O T H S. - Romans 15:13

Adoration

I will exalt you, my God and King, and praise your name forever and ever. I will praise you every day; yes, I will praise you forever. Great is the Lord! He is most worthy of praise! No one can measure his greatness.
Psalm 145:1-3

Confession

Have mercy on me, O God, because of your unfailing love. Because of your great compassion, blot out the stain of my sins. Wash me clean from my guilt. Purify me from my sin. For I recognize my rebellion; it haunts me day and night.
Psalm 51:1-3

Thanksgiving

Since we are receiving a Kingdom that is unshakable, let us be thankful and please God by worshiping him with holy fear and awe.
Hebrews 12:18

I W E Y, M G A K, A P Y N F A E. I W P Y E D; Y, I W P Y F. G I T L!
H I M W O P! N O C M H G. - Psalm 145:1-3

H M O M, O G, B O Y U L, B O Y G C, B O T S O M S. W M C F M G.
P M F M S. F I R M R; I H M D A N. - Psalm 51:1-3

S W A R A K T I U, L U B T A P G B W H W H F A A. - Hebrews 12:18

Children

....That their hearts may be encouraged, being knit together in love, to reach all the riches of full assurance of understanding and the knowledge of God's mystery, which is Christ.
Colossians 2:2

Marriages

Do not let any unwholesome talk come out of your mouths, but only what is helpful for building others up according to their needs, that it may benefit those who listen.
Ephesians 4:29

Finances & Stewardship

Whoever loves money never has enough; whoever loves wealth is never satisfied with their income. This too is meaningless.
Ecclesiastes 5:10

...TTHMBE, BKTIL, TRATROFAOUATKOGM, WIC. - Colossians 2:2

DNLAUTCOOYM, BOWIHFBOUATTN, TIMBTWL. - Ephesians 4:29

WLMNHE; WLWINSWTI. TTIM. - Ecclesiastes 5:10

The Church

A new commandment I give to you,
that you love one another: just as I have
loved you, you also are to love one another.
By this all people will know that you are
my disciples, if you have love
for one another.
John 13:34-35

Nations & Leaders

What joy for the nation whose God
is the Lord, whose people he
has chosen as his inheritance.
Psalm 33:12

Missionaries

But you should keep a clear mind in
every situation. Don't be afraid of suffering
for the Lord. Work at telling others the
Good News, and fully carry out the
ministry God has given you.
2 Timothy 4:5

ANCIGTOY,TYLOA:JAIHLY,YAATLOA.
BTAPWKTYAMD,IYHLFOA. - John 13:34-35

WJFTNWGITL,WPHHCAHI. - Psalm 33:12

BYSKACMIES.DBAOSFTL.WATOTGN,AFCOTMGHGY. - 2 Timothy 4:5

The Lost

Gently instruct those who oppose the truth. Perhaps God will change those people's hearts, and they will learn the truth. Then they will come to their senses and escape from the devil's trap. For they have been held captive by him to do whatever he wants.
2 Timothy 2:25-26

The Sick, Weary & Discouraged

I have told you these things, so that in me you may have peace. In this world you will have trouble. But take heart! I have overcome the world.
John 16:33

The Oppressed & Enslaved

When I am afraid, I put my trust in you. In God, whose word I praise—in God I trust and am not afraid. What can mere mortals do to me?
Psalm 56:3-4

GITWOTT.PGWCTPH, ATWLTT.TTWCTTS AEFTDT.FTHBHCBHTDWHW. - 2 Timothy 2:25-26

IHTYTT, STIMYMHP.ITWYWHT.BTH! IHOTW. - John 16:33

WIAA, IPMTIY.IG, WWIP - IGITAANA.WCMMDTM? - Psalm 56:3-4

Wisdom

Be very careful, then, how you live—
not as unwise but as wise, making the
most of every opportunity, because
the days are evil.
Ephesians 5:15-16

Daily Walk

Since, then, you have been raised with
Christ, set your hearts on things above,
where Christ is, seated at the right hand
of God. Set your minds on things above,
not on earthly things. For you
died, and your life is now
hidden with Christ in God.
Colossians 3:1-3

Gratitude & Joy

You make known to me the path of
life; in your presence there is
fullness of joy; at your right
hand are pleasures forevermore.
Psalm 16:11

B V C, T, H Y L - N A U B A W, M T M O E O, B T D A E. - Ephesians 5:15-16

S, T, Y H B R W C, S Y H O T A, W C I, S A T R H O G. S Y M O T A,
N O E T. F Y D, A Y L I N H W C I G. - Colossians 3:1-3

Y M K T M T P O L; I Y P T I F O J; A Y R H A P F. - Psalm 16:11

Adoration

Because your love is better than life, my lips will glorify you. I will praise you as long as I live, and in your name I will lift up my hands. I will be fully satisfied as with the richest of foods; with singing lips my mouth will praise you.
Psalm 63: 3-5

Confession

Whoever conceals their sins does not prosper, but the one who confesses and renounces them finds mercy.
Proverbs 28:13

Thanksgiving

Rejoice always, pray continually, give thanks in all circumstances; for this is God's will for you in Christ Jesus.
1 Thessalonians 5:16-18

BYLIBTL, MLWGY. IWPYALAIL, AIYNIWLUMH. IW BFSAWTROF; WSLMMWPY. - Psalm 63:3-5

WCTSDNP, BTOWCARTFM. - Proverbs 28:13

RA, PC, GTIAC; FTIGWFYICJ. - 1 Thessalonians 5:16-18

Children

May the Lord bless you and protect you. May the Lord smile on you and be gracious to you. May the Lord show you his favor and give you his peace.
Numbers 6:24-26

Marriages

May God, who gives this patience and encouragement, help you live in complete harmony with each other, as is fitting for followers of Christ Jesus. Then all of you can join together with one voice, giving praise and glory to God, the Father of our Lord Jesus Christ.
Romans 15:5-6

Finances & Stewardship

Keep your lives free from the love of money and be content with what you have, because God has said, "Never will I leave you; never will I forsake you."
Hebrews 13:5

M T L B Y A P Y. M T L S O Y A B G T Y. M T L S Y H F A G Y H P. - Numbers 6:24-26

M G, W G T P A E, H Y L I C H W E O, A I F F F O C J. T A O Y C J T W O V, G P A G T G, T F O O L J C. - Romans 15:5-6

K Y L F F T L O M A B C W W Y H, B G H S, "N W I L Y; N W I F Y." - Hebrews 13:5

The Church

If my people who are called by my name humble themselves, and pray and seek my face and turn from their wicked ways, then I will hear from heaven and will forgive their sin and heal their land.
2 Chronicles 7:14

Nations & Leaders

For our struggle is not against flesh and blood, but against the rulers, against the authorities, against the powers of this dark world and against the spiritual forces of evil in the heavenly realms.
Ephesians 6:12

Missionaries

Then he said to his disciples, "The harvest is plentiful but the workers are few. Ask the Lord of the harvest, therefore, to send out workers into his harvest field."
Matthew 9:27-28

I M P W A C B M N H T, A P A S M F A T F T W W, T I W H F H A W F T S A H T L. - 2 Chronicles 7:14

F O S I N A F A B, B A T R, A T A, A T P O T D W A A T S F O E I T H R. - Ephesians 6:12

T H S T H D, "T H I P B T W A F. A T L O T H, T, T S O W I H H F. - Matthew 9:27-28

The Lost

No one can come to me unless the Father who sent me draws them, and I will raise them up at the last day. It is written in the Prophets: 'They will all be taught by God.'
John 6:44-45

The Sick, Weary & Discouraged

The Lord gives strength to his people; the Lord blesses his people with peace.
Psalm 29:11

The Oppressed & Enslaved

The Lord is good, a strong refuge when trouble comes. He is close to those who trust in him. But he will sweep away his enemies in an overwhelming flood. He will pursue his foes into the darkness of night.
Nahum 1:7-8

N O C C T M U T F W S M D T, A I W R T U A T L D. I I W I T P: 'T W A B T B G.' - John 6:44-45

T L G S T H P; T L B H P W P. - Psalm 29:11

T L I G, A S R W T C. H I C T T W T I H. B H W S A H E I A O F. H W P H F I T D O N. - Nahum 1:7-8

Wisdom

If you are wise and understand God's ways, prove it by living an honorable life, doing good works with the humility that comes from wisdom.
James 3:13

Daily Walk

Beloved, let us love one another, for love is from God, and whoever loves has been born of God and knows God.
1 John 4:7

Gratitude & Joy

The commandments of the Lord are right, bringing joy to the heart. The commands of the Lord are clear, giving insight for living.
Psalm 19:8

I Y A W A U G W, P I B L A H L, D G W W T H T C F W. - James 3:13

B, L U L O A, F L I F G, A W L H B B O G A K G. - 1 John 4:7

T C O T L A R, B J T T H. T C O T L A C, G I F L. - Psalm 19:8

Adoration

I will extol you, my God and King, and bless your name forever and ever. Every day I will bless you and praise your name forever and ever. Great is the Lord, and greatly to be praised, and his greatness is unsearchable.
Psalm 145:1-3

Confession

Or do you show contempt for the riches of his kindness, forbearance and patience, not realizing that God's kindness is intended to lead you to repentance?
Romans 2:4

Thanksgiving

The Lord is my strength and my shield; my heart trusts in him, and he helps me. My heart leaps for joy, and with my song I praise him.
Psalm 28:7

I W E Y, M G A K, A B Y N F A E. E D I W B Y A P Y N F A E.
G I T L, A G T B P, A H G I U. - Psalm 145:1-3

O D Y S C F T R O H K, F A P, N R T G K I I T L Y T R? - Romans 2:4

T L I M S A M S; M H T I H, A H H M. M H L F J, A W M S I P H. - Psalm 28:7

Children

Do not conform to the pattern of this world, but be transformed by the renewing of your mind. Then you will be able to test and approve what God's will is—his good, pleasing and perfect will.
Romans 12:1-2

Marriages

Do nothing from selfish ambition or conceit, but in humility count others more significant than yourselves. Let each of you look not only to his own interests, but also to the interests of others.
Philippians 2:4-5

Finances & Stewardship

But godliness with contentment is great gain. For we brought nothing into the world, and we can take nothing out of it. But if we have food and clothing, we will be content with that.
1 Timothy 6:6-8

D N C T T P O T W, B B T B T R O Y M. T Y W B A T T A A W G W I - H G, P A P W. - Romans 12:1-2

D N F S A O C, B I H C O M S T Y. L E O Y L N O T H O I, B A T T I O O. - Philippians 2:4-5

B G W C I G G. F W B N I T W, A W C T N O O I. B I
W H F A C, W W B C W T. 1 Timothy 6:6-8

The Church

May the God who gives endurance and encouragement give you the same attitude of mind toward each other that Christ Jesus had, so that with one mind and one voice you may glorify the God and Father of our Lord Jesus Christ.
Romans 15:5

Nations & Leaders

The fear of the Lord is the beginning of wisdom, and the knowledge of the Holy One is insight.
Proverbs 9:10

Missionaries

It's not important who does the planting, or who does the watering. What's important is that God makes the seed grow. The one who plants and the one who waters work together with the same purpose. And both will be rewarded for their own hard work.
1 Corinthians 3:7-8

MTGWGEAEGYTSAOMTEOTCJH, STWO MAOVYMGTGAFOOLJC. - Romans 15:5

TFOTLITBOW, ATKOTHOII. - Proverbs 9:10

INIWDTP, OWDTW. WIITGMTSG. TOWPATOWWWTW TSP. ABWBRFTOHW. - 1 Corinthians 3:7-8

The Lost

If you declare with your mouth, "Jesus is Lord," and believe in your heart that God raised him from the dead, you will be saved. For it is with your heart that you believe and are justified, and it is with your mouth that you profess your faith and are saved.
Romans 10:9-10

The Sick, Weary & Discouraged

Do not be anxious about anything, but in everything by prayer and supplication with thanksgiving let your requests be made known to God. And the peace of God, which surpasses all understanding, will guard your hearts and your minds in Christ Jesus.
Philippians 4:6-7

The Oppressed & Enslaved

But as for me, I shall sing of Your strength; Yes, I shall joyfully sing of Your lovingkindness in the morning, For You have been my stronghold And a refuge in the day of my distress.
Psalm 59:16

I Y D W Y M, "J I L," A B I Y H T G R H F T D, Y W B S. F I I W Y H T Y B A A J, A I I W Y M T Y P Y F A A S. - Romans 10:9-10

D N B A A A, B I E B P A S W T L Y R B M K T G. A T P O G, W S A U, W G Y H A Y M I C J. - Philippians 4:6-7

B A F M, I S S O Y S; Y, I S J S O Y L I T M, F Y H B M S A A R I T D O M D. - Psalm 59:16

Wisdom

Everyone then who hears these words of mine and does them will be like a wise man who built his house on the rock.
Matthew 7:24

Daily Walk

But I say, walk by the Spirit, and you will not gratify the desires of the flesh.
Galatians 5:16

Gratitude & Joy

Instead, be filled with the Spirit, speaking to one another with psalms, hymns, and songs from the Spirit. Sing and make music from your heart to the Lord, always giving thanks to God the Father for everything, in the name of our Lord Jesus Christ.
Ephesians 5:18b-20

E T W H T W O M A D T W B L A W M W B H H O T R. - Matthew 7:24

B I S, W B T S, A Y W N G T D O T F. - Galatians 5:16

I, B F W T S, S T O A W P, H, A S F T S. S A M M F Y H T T L, A G T T G T F F E, I T N O O L J C. - Ephesians 5:18b-20

Adoration

Great and marvelous are your deeds, Lord God Almighty. Just and true are your ways, King of the nations. Who will not fear you, Lord, and bring glory to your name? For you alone are holy. All nations will come and worship before you, for your righteous acts have been revealed.
Revelation 15:3b-4

Confession

Those whom I love I rebuke and discipline. So be earnest and repent. Here I am! I stand at the door and knock. If anyone hears my voice and opens the door, I will come in and eat with that person, and they with me.
Revelation 3:19-20

Thanksgiving

Every good and perfect gift is from above, coming down from the Father of the heavenly lights, who does not change like shifting shadows.
James 1:17

GAMAYD, LGA. JATAYW, KOTN. WWNFY, L, ABGT YN? FYAAH. ANWCAWBY, FYRAHBR. - Revelation 15:3b-4

TWILIRAD. SBEAR. HIA! ISATDAK. IAHMVAOTD, IWCIAEWTP, ATWM. - Revelation 3:19-20

EGAPGIFA, CDFTFOTHL, WDNCLSS. - James 1:17

Children

Behold, children are a gift of the Lord. The fruit of the womb is a reward. Like arrows in the hand of a warrior, so are the children of one's youth.
Psalm 127:3-4

Marriages

Two are better than one, because they have a good reward for their labor. For if they fall, one will lift up his companion. But woe to him who is alone when he falls, for he has no one to help him up.
Ecclesiastes 4:9-10

Finances & Stewardship

Choose a good reputation over great riches; being held in high esteem is better than silver or gold. The rich and poor have this in common: The Lord made them both.
Proverbs 22:1-2

B, C A A G O T L. T F O T W I A R. L A I T H O A W, S A T C O O Y. - Psalm 127:3-4

T A B T O, B T H A G R F T L. F I T F, O W L U H C. B W T H W I A W H F, F H H N O T H H U. - Ecclesiastes 4:9-10

C A G R O G R; B H I H E I B T S O G. T R A P H T I C: T L M T B. - Proverbs 22:1-2

The Church

God is spirit, and those who worship him must worship in spirit and truth.
John 4:24

Nations & Leaders

The king's heart is a stream of water in the hand of the Lord; he turns it wherever he will.
Proverbs 21:1

Missionaries

Preach the word of God. Be prepared, whether the time is favorable or not. Patiently correct, rebuke, and encourage your people with good teaching.
2 Timothy 4:2

G I S, A T W W H M W I S A T. - John 4:24

T K H I A S O W I T H O T L; H T I W H W. - Proverbs 21:1

P T W O G. B P, W T T I F O N. P C, R, A E Y P W G T. - 2 Timothy 4:2

The Lost

And I will give them one heart, and a new spirit I will put within them. I will remove the heart of stone from their flesh and give them a heart of flesh, that they may walk in my statutes and keep my rules and obey them. And they shall be my people, and I will be their God.
Ezekiel 11:19-20

The Sick, Weary & Discouraged

Fear not, for I am with you; be not dismayed, for I am your God; I will strengthen you, I will help you, I will uphold you with my righteous right hand.
Isaiah 41:10

The Oppressed & Enslaved

The Spirit of the Lord is upon me, because he has anointed me to proclaim good news to the poor. He has sent me to proclaim liberty to the captives and recovering of sight to the blind, to set at liberty those who are oppressed.
Luke 4:18

A I W G T O H, A A N S I W P W T. I W R T H O S F T F A G T A H O F, T T M W I M S A K M R A O T. A T S B M P, A I W B T G. - Ezekiel 11:19-20

F N, F I A W Y; B N D, F I A Y G; I W S Y, I W H Y, I W U Y W M R R H. - Isaiah 41:10

T S O T L I U M, B H H A M T P G N T T P. H H S M T P L T T C A R O S T T B, T S A L T W A O. - Luke 4:18

Wisdom

Don't be impressed with your own wisdom. Instead, fear the Lord and turn away from evil. Then you will have healing for your body and strength for your bones.
Proverbs 3:7-8

Daily Walk

Take delight in the Lord, and he will give you your heart's desires. Commit everything you do to the Lord. Trust him, and he will help you.
Psalm 7:4-5

Gratitude & Joy

I pray that God, the source of hope, will fill you completely with joy and peace because you trust in him. Then you will overflow with confident hope through the power of the Holy Spirit.
Romans 15:13

D B I W Y O W. I, F T L A T A F E. T Y W H H F Y B A S F Y B. - Proverbs 3:7-8

T D I T L, A H W G Y Y H D. C E Y D T T L. T H, A H W H Y. - Psalm 7:4-5

I P T G, T S O H, W F Y C W J A P B Y T I H. T Y W O W C H T T P O T H S. - Romans 15:13

Adoration

I will exalt you, my God and King, and praise your name forever and ever. I will praise you every day; yes, I will praise you forever. Great is the Lord! He is most worthy of praise! No one can measure his greatness.
Psalm 145:1-3

Confession

Have mercy on me, O God, because of your unfailing love. Because of your great compassion, blot out the stain of my sins. Wash me clean from my guilt. Purify me from my sin. For I recognize my rebellion; it haunts me day and night.
Psalm 51:1-3

Thanksgiving

Since we are receiving a Kingdom that is unshakable, let us be thankful and please God by worshiping him with holy fear and awe.
Hebrews 12:18

IWEY,MGAK,APYNFAE.IWPYED;Y,IWPYF.GITL!
HIMWOP!NOCMHG. - Psalm 145:1-3

HMOM,OG,BOYUL,BOYGC,BOTSOMS.WMCFMG.
PMFMS.FIRMR;IHMDAN. - Psalm 51:1-3

SWARAKTIU,LUBTAPGBWHWHFAA. - Hebrews 12:18

Children

....That their hearts may be encouraged, being knit together in love, to reach all the riches of full assurance of understanding and the knowledge of God's mystery, which is Christ.
Colossians 2:2

Marriages

Do not let any unwholesome talk come out of your mouths, but only what is helpful for building others up according to their needs, that it may benefit those who listen.
Ephesians 4:29

Finances & Stewardship

Whoever loves money never has enough; whoever loves wealth is never satisfied with their income. This too is meaningless.
Ecclesiastes 5:10

...TTHMBE, BKTIL, TRATROFAOUATKOGM, WIC. - Colossians 2:2

DNLAUTCOOYM, BOWIHFBOUATTN, TIMBTWL. - Ephesians 4:29

WLMNHE; WLWINSWTI. TTIM. - Ecclesiastes 5:10

The Church

A new commandment I give to you, that you love one another: just as I have loved you, you also are to love one another. By this all people will know that you are my disciples, if you have love for one another.
John 13:34-35

Nations & Leaders

What joy for the nation whose God is the Lord, whose people he has chosen as his inheritance.
Psalm 33:12

Missionaries

But you should keep a clear mind in every situation. Don't be afraid of suffering for the Lord. Work at telling others the Good News, and fully carry out the ministry God has given you.
2 Timothy 4:5

A N C I G T O Y, T Y L O A: J A I H L Y, Y A A T L O A. B T A P W K T Y A M D, I Y H L F O A. - John 13:34-35

W J F T N W G I T L, W P H H C A H I. - Psalm 33:12

B Y S K A C M I E S. D B A O S F T L. W A T O T G N, A F C O T M G H G Y. - 2 Timothy 4:5

The Lost

Gently instruct those who oppose the truth. Perhaps God will change those people's hearts, and they will learn the truth. Then they will come to their senses and escape from the devil's trap. For they have been held captive by him to do whatever he wants.
2 Timothy 2:25-26

The Sick, Weary & Discouraged

I have told you these things, so that in me you may have peace. In this world you will have trouble. But take heart! I have overcome the world.
John 16:33

The Oppressed & Enslaved

When I am afraid, I put my trust in you. In God, whose word I praise—in God I trust and am not afraid. What can mere mortals do to me?
Psalm 56:3-4

GITWOTT.PGWCTPH, ATWLTT.TTWCTTS AEFTDT.FTHBHCBHTDWHW. - 2 Timothy 2:25-26

IHTYTT, STIMYMHP.ITWYWHT. BTH! IHOTW. - John 16:33

WIAA, IPMTIY.IG, WWIP - IGITAANA.WCMMDTM? - Psalm 56:3-4

Wisdom

Be very careful, then, how you live—not as unwise but as wise, making the most of every opportunity, because the days are evil.
Ephesians 5:15-16

Daily Walk

Since, then, you have been raised with Christ, set your hearts on things above, where Christ is, seated at the right hand of God. Set your minds on things above, not on earthly things. For you died, and your life is now hidden with Christ in God.
Colossians 3:1-3

Gratitude & Joy

You make known to me the path of life; in your presence there is fullness of joy; at your right hand are pleasures forevermore.
Psalm 16:11

B V C, T, H Y L - N A U B A W, M T M O E O, B T D A E. - Ephesians 5:15-16

S, T, Y H B R W C, S Y H O T A, W C I, S A T R H O G. S Y M O T A, N O E T. F Y D, A Y L I N H W C I G. - Colossians 3:1-3

Y M K T M T P O L; I Y P T I F O J; A Y R H A P F. - Psalm 16:11

Adoration

Because your love is better than life, my lips will glorify you. I will praise you as long as I live, and in your name I will lift up my hands. I will be fully satisfied as with the richest of foods; with singing lips my mouth will praise you.
Psalm 63: 3-5

Confession

Whoever conceals their sins does not prosper, but the one who confesses and renounces them finds mercy.
Proverbs 28:13

Thanksgiving

Rejoice always, pray continually, give thanks in all circumstances; for this is God's will for you in Christ Jesus.
1 Thessalonians 5:16-18

BYLIBTL, MLWGY. IWPYALAIL, AIYNIWLUMH. IW BFSAWTROF; WSLMMWPY. - Psalm 63:3-5

WCTSDNP, BTOWCARTFM. - Proverbs 28:13

RA, PC, GTIAC; FTIGWFYICJ. - 1 Thessalonians 5:16-18

Children

May the Lord bless you and protect you. May the Lord smile on you and be gracious to you. May the Lord show you his favor and give you his peace.
Numbers 6:24-26

Marriages

May God, who gives this patience and encouragement, help you live in complete harmony with each other, as is fitting for followers of Christ Jesus. Then all of you can join together with one voice, giving praise and glory to God, the Father of our Lord Jesus Christ.
Romans 15:5-6

Finances & Stewardship

Keep your lives free from the love of money and be content with what you have, because God has said, "Never will I leave you; never will I forsake you."
Hebrews 13:5

MTLBYAPY. MTLSOYABGTY. MTLSYHFAGYHP. - Numbers 6:24-26

MG, WGTPAE, HYLICHWEO, AIFFFOCJ. TAOYCJTW OV, GPAGTG, TFOOLJC. - Romans 15:5-6

KYLFFTLOMABCWWYH, BGHS, "NWILY; NWIFY." - Hebrews 13:5

The Church

If my people who are called by my name humble themselves, and pray and seek my face and turn from their wicked ways, then I will hear from heaven and will forgive their sin and heal their land.
2 Chronicles 7:14

Nations & Leaders

For our struggle is not against flesh and blood, but against the rulers, against the authorities, against the powers of this dark world and against the spiritual forces of evil in the heavenly realms.
Ephesians 6:12

Missionaries

Then he said to his disciples, "The harvest is plentiful but the workers are few. Ask the Lord of the harvest, therefore, to send out workers into his harvest field."
Matthew 9:27-28

I M P W A C B M N H T, A P A S M F A T F T W W, T I W H F H A W F T S A H T L. - 2 Chronicles 7:14

F O S I N A F A B, B A T R, A T A, A T P O T D W A A T S F O E I T H R. - Ephesians 6:12

T H S T H D, "T H I P B T W A F. A T L O T H, T, T S O W I H H F. - Matthew 9:27-28

The Lost

No one can come to me unless the Father who sent me draws them, and I will raise them up at the last day. It is written in the Prophets: 'They will all be taught by God.'
John 6:44-45

The Sick, Weary & Discouraged

The Lord gives strength to his people; the Lord blesses his people with peace.
Psalm 29:11

The Oppressed & Enslaved

The Lord is good, a strong refuge when trouble comes. He is close to those who trust in him. But he will sweep away his enemies in an overwhelming flood. He will pursue his foes into the darkness of night.
Nahum 1:7-8

N O C C T M U T F W S M D T, A I W R T U A T L D. I I W I T P: 'T W A B T B G.' - John 6:44-45

T L G S T H P; T L B H P W P. - Psalm 29:11

T L I G, A S R W T C. H I C T T W T I H. B H W S A H E I
A O F. H W P H F I T D O N. - Nahum 1:7-8

Wisdom

If you are wise and understand God's ways, prove it by living an honorable life, doing good works with the humility that comes from wisdom.
James 3:13

Daily Walk

Beloved, let us love one another, for love is from God, and whoever loves has been born of God and knows God.
1 John 4:7

Gratitude & Joy

The commandments of the Lord are right, bringing joy to the heart. The commands of the Lord are clear, giving insight for living.
Psalm 19:8

I Y A W A U G W, P I B L A H L, D G W W T H T C F W. - James 3:13

B, L U L O A, F L I F G, A W L H B B O G A K G. - 1 John 4:7

T C O T L A R, B J T T H. T C O T L A C, G I F L. - Psalm 19:8

Adoration

I will extol you, my God and King, and bless your name forever and ever. Every day I will bless you and praise your name forever and ever. Great is the Lord, and greatly to be praised, and his greatness is unsearchable.
Psalm 145:1-3

Confession

Or do you show contempt for the riches of his kindness, forbearance and patience, not realizing that God's kindness is intended to lead you to repentance?
Romans 2:4

Thanksgiving

The Lord is my strength and my shield; my heart trusts in him, and he helps me. My heart leaps for joy, and with my song I praise him.
Psalm 28:7

I W E Y, M G A K, A B Y N F A E. E D I W B Y A P Y N F A E.
G I T L, A G T B P, A H G I U. - Psalm 145:1-3

O D Y S C F T R O H K, F A P, N R T G K I I T L Y T R? - Romans 2:4

T L I M S A M S; M H T I H, A H H M. M H L F J, A W M S I P H. - Psalm 28:7

Children

Do not conform to the pattern of this world, but be transformed by the renewing of your mind. Then you will be able to test and approve what God's will is—his good, pleasing and perfect will.
Romans 12:1-2

Marriages

Do nothing from selfish ambition or conceit, but in humility count others more significant than yourselves. Let each of you look not only to his own interests, but also to the interests of others.
Philippians 2:4-5

Finances & Stewardship

But godliness with contentment is great gain. For we brought nothing into the world, and we can take nothing out of it. But if we have food and clothing, we will be content with that.
1 Timothy 6:6-8

D N C T T P O T W, B B T B T R O Y M. T Y W B A T T A A W G W I - H G, P A P W. - Romans 12:1-2

D N F S A O C, B I H C O M S T Y. L E O Y L N O T H O I, B A T T I O O. - Philippians 2:4-5

B G W C I G G. F W B N I T W, A W C T N O O I. B I
W H F A C, W W B C W T. 1 Timothy 6:6-8

The Church

May the God who gives endurance and encouragement give you the same attitude of mind toward each other that Christ Jesus had, so that with one mind and one voice you may glorify the God and Father of our Lord Jesus Christ.
Romans 15:5

Nations & Leaders

The fear of the Lord is the beginning of wisdom, and the knowledge of the Holy One is insight.
Proverbs 9:10

Missionaries

It's not important who does the planting, or who does the watering. What's important is that God makes the seed grow. The one who plants and the one who waters work together with the same purpose. And both will be rewarded for their own hard work.
1 Corinthians 3:7-8

MTGWGEAEGYTSAOMTEOTCJH, STWO MAOVYMGTGAFOOLJC. - Romans 15:5

TFOTLITBOW, ATKOTHOII. - Proverbs 9:10

INIWDTP, OWDTW. WIITGMTSG. TOWPATOWWWTW TSP. ABWBRFTOHW. - 1 Corinthians 3:7-8

The Lost

If you declare with your mouth, "Jesus is Lord," and believe in your heart that God raised him from the dead, you will be saved. For it is with your heart that you believe and are justified, and it is with your mouth that you profess your faith and are saved.
Romans 10:9-10

The Sick, Weary & Discouraged

Do not be anxious about anything, but in everything by prayer and supplication with thanksgiving let your requests be made known to God. And the peace of God, which surpasses all understanding, will guard your hearts and your minds in Christ Jesus.
Philippians 4:6-7

The Oppressed & Enslaved

But as for me, I shall sing of Your strength; Yes, I shall joyfully sing of Your lovingkindness in the morning, For You have been my stronghold And a refuge in the day of my distress.
Psalm 59:16

IYDWYM, "JIL," ABIYHTGRHFTD, YWBS. FIIWYHT YBAAJ, AIIWYMTYPYFAAS. - Romans 10:9-10

DNBAAA, BIEBPASWTLYRBMKTG. ATPOG, WSAU, WGYHAYMICJ. - Philippians 4:6-7

BAFM, ISSOYS; Y, ISJSOYLITM, FYHBMSAARITDOMD. - Psalm 59:16

Wisdom

Everyone then who hears these words of mine and does them will be like a wise man who built his house on the rock.
Matthew 7:24

Daily Walk

But I say, walk by the Spirit, and you will not gratify the desires of the flesh.
Galatians 5:16

Gratitude & Joy

Instead, be filled with the Spirit, speaking to one another with psalms, hymns, and songs from the Spirit. Sing and make music from your heart to the Lord, always giving thanks to God the Father for everything, in the name of our Lord Jesus Christ.
Ephesians 5:18b-20

ETWHTWOMADTWBLAWMWBHHOTR. - Matthew 7:24

BIS, WBTS, AYWNGTDOTF. - Galatians 5:16

I, BFWTS, STOAWP, H, ASFTS. SAMMFYHTTL, AGTTGTFFE, ITNOOLJC. - Ephesians 5:18b-20

Adoration

Great and marvelous are your deeds, Lord God Almighty. Just and true are your ways, King of the nations. Who will not fear you, Lord, and bring glory to your name? For you alone are holy. All nations will come and worship before you, for your righteous acts have been revealed.
Revelation 15:3b-4

Confession

Those whom I love I rebuke and discipline. So be earnest and repent. Here I am! I stand at the door and knock. If anyone hears my voice and opens the door, I will come in and eat with that person, and they with me.
Revelation 3:19-20

Thanksgiving

Every good and perfect gift is from above, coming down from the Father of the heavenly lights, who does not change like shifting shadows.
James 1:17

G A M A Y D, L G A. J A T A Y W, K O T N. W W N F Y, L, A B G T Y N? F Y A A H. A N W C A W B Y, F Y R A H B R. - Revelation 15:3b-4

T W I L I R A D. S B E A R. H I A! I S A T D A K. I A H M V A O T D, I W C I A E W T P, A T W M. - Revelation 3:19-20

E G A P G I F A, C D F T F O T H L, W D N C L S S. - James 1:17

Children

Behold, children are a gift of the Lord. The fruit of the womb is a reward. Like arrows in the hand of a warrior, so are the children of one's youth.
Psalm 127:3-4

Marriages

Two are better than one, because they have a good reward for their labor. For if they fall, one will lift up his companion. But woe to him who is alone when he falls, for he has no one to help him up.
Ecclesiastes 4:9-10

Finances & Stewardship

Choose a good reputation over great riches; being held in high esteem is better than silver or gold. The rich and poor have this in common: The Lord made them both.
Proverbs 22:1-2

B, C A A G O T L. T F O T W I A R. L A I T H O A W, S A T C O O Y. - Psalm 127:3-4

T A B T O, B T H A G R F T L. F I T F, O W L U H C. B W T H W I A W H F, F H H N O T H H U. - Ecclesiastes 4:9-10

C A G R O G R; B H I H E I B T S O G. T R A P H T I C: T L M T B. - Proverbs 22:1-2

The Church

God is spirit, and those who worship him must worship in spirit and truth.
John 4:24

Nations & Leaders

The king's heart is a stream of water in the hand of the Lord; he turns it wherever he will.
Proverbs 21:1

Missionaries

Preach the word of God. Be prepared, whether the time is favorable or not. Patiently correct, rebuke, and encourage your people with good teaching.
2 Timothy 4:2

G I S, A T W W H M W I S A T. - John 4:24

T K H I A S O W I T H O T L; H T I W H W. - Proverbs 21:1

P T W O G. B P, W T T I F O N. P C, R, A E Y P W G T. - 2 Timothy 4:2

The Lost

And I will give them one heart, and a new spirit I will put within them. I will remove the heart of stone from their flesh and give them a heart of flesh, that they may walk in my statutes and keep my rules and obey them. And they shall be my people, and I will be their God.
Ezekiel 11:19-20

The Sick, Weary & Discouraged

Fear not, for I am with you; be not dismayed, for I am your God; I will strengthen you, I will help you, I will uphold you with my righteous right hand.
Isaiah 41:10

The Oppressed & Enslaved

The Spirit of the Lord is upon me, because he has anointed me to proclaim good news to the poor. He has sent me to proclaim liberty to the captives and recovering of sight to the blind, to set at liberty those who are oppressed.
Luke 4:18

AIWGTOH, AANSIWPWT. IWRTHOSFTFAGTAHOF, TTMWIMSAKMRAOT. ATSBMP, AIWBTG. - Ezekiel 11:19-20

FN, FIAWY; BND, FIAYG; IWSY, IWHY, IWUYWMRRH. - Isaiah 41:10

TSOTLIUM, BHHAMTPGNTTP. HHSMT PLTTCAROSTTB, TSALTWAO. - Luke 4:18

Wisdom

Don't be impressed with your own wisdom. Instead, fear the Lord and turn away from evil. Then you will have healing for your body and strength for your bones.
Proverbs 3:7-8

Daily Walk

Take delight in the Lord, and he will give you your heart's desires. Commit everything you do to the Lord. Trust him, and he will help you.
Psalm 7:4-5

Gratitude & Joy

I pray that God, the source of hope, will fill you completely with joy and peace because you trust in him. Then you will overflow with confident hope through the power of the Holy Spirit.
Romans 15:13

D B I W Y O W. I, F T L A T A F E. T Y W H H F Y B A S F Y B. - Proverbs 3:7-8

T D I T L, A H W G Y Y H D. C E Y D T T L. T H, A H W H Y. - Psalm 7:4-5

I P T G, T S O H, W F Y C W J A P B Y T I H. T Y W O W C H T T P O T H S. - Romans 15:13

Adoration

I will exalt you, my God and King, and praise your name forever and ever. I will praise you every day; yes, I will praise you forever. Great is the Lord! He is most worthy of praise! No one can measure his greatness.
Psalm 145:1-3

Confession

Have mercy on me, O God, because of your unfailing love. Because of your great compassion, blot out the stain of my sins. Wash me clean from my guilt. Purify me from my sin. For I recognize my rebellion; it haunts me day and night.
Psalm 51:1-3

Thanksgiving

Since we are receiving a Kingdom that is unshakable, let us be thankful and please God by worshiping him with holy fear and awe.
Hebrews 12:18

IWEY,MGAK,APYNFAE.IWPYED;Y,IWPYF.GITL!
HIMWOP!NOCMHG. - Psalm 145:1-3

HMOM,OG,BOYUL,BOYGC,BOTSOMS.WMCFMG.
PMFMS.FIRMR;IHMDAN. - Psalm 51:1-3

SWARAKTIU,LUBTAPGBWHWHFAA. - Hebrews 12:18

Children

....That their hearts may be encouraged, being knit together in love, to reach all the riches of full assurance of understanding and the knowledge of God's mystery, which is Christ.
Colossians 2:2

Marriages

Do not let any unwholesome talk come out of your mouths, but only what is helpful for building others up according to their needs, that it may benefit those who listen.
Ephesians 4:29

Finances & Stewardship

Whoever loves money never has enough; whoever loves wealth is never satisfied with their income. This too is meaningless.
Ecclesiastes 5:10

...T T H M B E, B K T I L, T R A T R O F A O U A T K O G M, W I C. - Colossians 2:2

D N L A U T C O O Y M, B O W I H F B O U A T T N, T I M B T W L. - Ephesians 4:29

W L M N H E; W L W I N S W T I. T T I M. - Ecclesiastes 5:10

The Church

A new commandment I give to you, that you love one another: just as I have loved you, you also are to love one another. By this all people will know that you are my disciples, if you have love for one another.
John 13:34-35

Nations & Leaders

What joy for the nation whose God is the Lord, whose people he has chosen as his inheritance.
Psalm 33:12

Missionaries

But you should keep a clear mind in every situation. Don't be afraid of suffering for the Lord. Work at telling others the Good News, and fully carry out the ministry God has given you.
2 Timothy 4:5

A N C I G T O Y, T Y L O A: J A I H L Y, Y A A T L O A. B T A P W K T Y A M D, I Y H L F O A. - John 13:34-35

W J F T N W G I T L, W P H H C A H I. - Psalm 33:12

B Y S K A C M I E S. D B A O S F T L. W A T O T G N, A F C O T M G H G Y. - 2 Timothy 4:5

The Lost

Gently instruct those who oppose the truth. Perhaps God will change those people's hearts, and they will learn the truth. Then they will come to their senses and escape from the devil's trap. For they have been held captive by him to do whatever he wants.
2 Timothy 2:25-26

The Sick, Weary & Discouraged

I have told you these things, so that in me you may have peace. In this world you will have trouble. But take heart! I have overcome the world.
John 16:33

The Oppressed & Enslaved

When I am afraid, I put my trust in you. In God, whose word I praise—in God I trust and am not afraid. What can mere mortals do to me?
Psalm 56:3-4

GITWOTT. PGWCTPH, ATWLTT. TTWCTTS AEFTDT. FTHBHCBHTDWHW. - 2 Timothy 2:25-26

IHTYTT, STIMYMHP. ITWYWHT. BTH! IHOTW. - John 16:33

WIAA, IPMTIY. IG, WWIP - IGITAANA. WCMMDTM? - Psalm 56:3-4

Wisdom

Be very careful, then, how you live—not as unwise but as wise, making the most of every opportunity, because the days are evil.
Ephesians 5:15-16

Daily Walk

Since, then, you have been raised with Christ, set your hearts on things above, where Christ is, seated at the right hand of God. Set your minds on things above, not on earthly things. For you died, and your life is now hidden with Christ in God.
Colossians 3:1-3

Gratitude & Joy

You make known to me the path of life; in your presence there is fullness of joy; at your right hand are pleasures forevermore.
Psalm 16:11

B V C, T, H Y L - N A U B A W, M T M O E O, B T D A E. - Ephesians 5:15-16

S, T, Y H B R W C, S Y H O T A, W C I, S A T R H O G. S Y M O T A, N O E T. F Y D, A Y L I N H W C I G. - Colossians 3:1-3

Y M K T M T P O L; I Y P T I F O J; A Y R H A P F. - Psalm 16:11

Adoration

Because your love is better than life, my lips will glorify you. I will praise you as long as I live, and in your name I will lift up my hands. I will be fully satisfied as with the richest of foods; with singing lips my mouth will praise you.
Psalm 63: 3-5

Confession

Whoever conceals their sins does not prosper, but the one who confesses and renounces them finds mercy.
Proverbs 28:13

Thanksgiving

Rejoice always, pray continually, give thanks in all circumstances; for this is God's will for you in Christ Jesus.
1 Thessalonians 5:16-18

B Y L I B T L, M L W G Y. I W P Y A L A I L, A I Y N I W L U M H. I W B F S A W T R O F; W S L M M W P Y. - Psalm 63:3-5

W C T S D N P, B T O W C A R T F M. - Proverbs 28:13

R A, P C, G T I A C; F T I G W F Y I C J. - 1 Thessalonians 5:16-18

Children

May the Lord bless you and protect you. May the Lord smile on you and be gracious to you. May the Lord show you his favor and give you his peace.
Numbers 6:24-26

Marriages

May God, who gives this patience and encouragement, help you live in complete harmony with each other, as is fitting for followers of Christ Jesus. Then all of you can join together with one voice, giving praise and glory to God, the Father of our Lord Jesus Christ.
Romans 15:5-6

Finances & Stewardship

Keep your lives free from the love of money and be content with what you have, because God has said, "Never will I leave you; never will I forsake you."
Hebrews 13:5

M T L B Y A P Y. M T L S O Y A B G T Y. M T L S Y H F A G Y H P. - Numbers 6:24-26

M G, W G T P A E, H Y L I C H W E O, A I F F F O C J. T A O Y C J T W O V, G P A G T G, T F O O L J C. - Romans 15:5-6

K Y L F F T L O M A B C W W Y H, B G H S, "N W I L Y; N W I F Y." - Hebrews 13:5

The Church

If my people who are called by my name humble themselves, and pray and seek my face and turn from their wicked ways, then I will hear from heaven and will forgive their sin and heal their land.
2 Chronicles 7:14

Nations & Leaders

For our struggle is not against flesh and blood, but against the rulers, against the authorities, against the powers of this dark world and against the spiritual forces of evil in the heavenly realms.
Ephesians 6:12

Missionaries

Then he said to his disciples, "The harvest is plentiful but the workers are few. Ask the Lord of the harvest, therefore, to send out workers into his harvest field."
Matthew 9:27-28

IMPWACBMNHT, APASMFATFTWW, TIWHFHAWFTSAHTL. - 2 Chronicles 7:14

FOSINAFAB, BATR, ATA, ATPOTDWAATSFOEITHR. - Ephesians 6:12

THSTHD, "THIPBTWAF. ATLOTH, T, TSOWIHHF. - Matthew 9:27-28

The Lost

No one can come to me unless the Father who sent me draws them, and I will raise them up at the last day. It is written in the Prophets: 'They will all be taught by God.'
John 6:44-45

The Sick, Weary & Discouraged

The Lord gives strength to his people; the Lord blesses his people with peace.
Psalm 29:11

The Oppressed & Enslaved

The Lord is good, a strong refuge when trouble comes. He is close to those who trust in him. But he will sweep away his enemies in an overwhelming flood. He will pursue his foes into the darkness of night.
Nahum 1:7-8

N O C C T M U T F W S M D T, A I W R T U A T L D. I I W I T P: 'T W A B T B G.' - John 6:44-45

T L G S T H P; T L B H P W P. - Psalm 29:11

T L I G, A S R W T C. H I C T T W T I H. B H W S A H E I
A O F. H W P H F I T D O N. - Nahum 1:7-8

Wisdom

If you are wise and understand God's ways, prove it by living an honorable life, doing good works with the humility that comes from wisdom.
James 3:13

Daily Walk

Beloved, let us love one another, for love is from God, and whoever loves has been born of God and knows God.
1 John 4:7

Gratitude & Joy

The commandments of the Lord are right, bringing joy to the heart. The commands of the Lord are clear, giving insight for living.
Psalm 19:8

I Y A W A U G W, P I B L A H L, D G W W T H T C F W. - James 3:13

B, L U L O A, F L I F G, A W L H B B O G A K G. - 1 John 4:7

T C O T L A R, B J T T H. T C O T L A C, G I F L. - Psalm 19:8

Adoration

I will extol you, my God and King, and bless your name forever and ever. Every day I will bless you and praise your name forever and ever. Great is the Lord, and greatly to be praised, and his greatness is unsearchable.
Psalm 145:1-3

Confession

Or do you show contempt for the riches of his kindness, forbearance and patience, not realizing that God's kindness is intended to lead you to repentance?
Romans 2:4

Thanksgiving

The Lord is my strength and my shield; my heart trusts in him, and he helps me. My heart leaps for joy, and with my song I praise him.
Psalm 28:7

I W E Y, M G A K, A B Y N F A E. E D I W B Y A P Y N F A E.
G I T L, A G T B P, A H G I U. - Psalm 145:1-3

O D Y S C F T R O H K, F A P, N R T G K I I T L Y T R? - Romans 2:4

T L I M S A M S; M H T I H, A H H M. M H L F J, A W M S I P H. - Psalm 28:7

Children

Do not conform to the pattern of this world, but be transformed by the renewing of your mind. Then you will be able to test and approve what God's will is—his good, pleasing and perfect will.
Romans 12:1-2

Marriages

Do nothing from selfish ambition or conceit, but in humility count others more significant than yourselves. Let each of you look not only to his own interests, but also to the interests of others.
Philippians 2:4-5

Finances & Stewardship

But godliness with contentment is great gain. For we brought nothing into the world, and we can take nothing out of it. But if we have food and clothing, we will be content with that.
1 Timothy 6:6-8

D N C T T P O T W, B B T B T R O Y M. T Y W B A T T A A W G W I - H G, P A P W. - Romans 12:1-2

D N F S A O C, B I H C O M S T Y. L E O Y L N O T H O I, B A T T I O O. - Philippians 2:4-5

B G W C I G G. F W B N I T W, A W C T N O O I. B I
W H F A C, W W B C W T. 1 Timothy 6:6-8

The Church

May the God who gives endurance and encouragement give you the same attitude of mind toward each other that Christ Jesus had, so that with one mind and one voice you may glorify the God and Father of our Lord Jesus Christ.
Romans 15:5

Nations & Leaders

The fear of the Lord is the beginning of wisdom, and the knowledge of the Holy One is insight.
Proverbs 9:10

Missionaries

It's not important who does the planting, or who does the watering. What's important is that God makes the seed grow. The one who plants and the one who waters work together with the same purpose. And both will be rewarded for their own hard work.
1 Corinthians 3:7-8

MTGWGEAEGYTSAOMTEOTCJH, STWO MAOVYMGTGAFOOLJC. - Romans 15:5

TFOTLITBOW, ATKOTHOII. - Proverbs 9:10

INIWDTP, OWDTW. WIITGMTSG. TOWPATOWWWTW TSP. ABWBRFTOHW. - 1 Corinthians 3:7-8

The Lost

If you declare with your mouth, "Jesus is Lord," and believe in your heart that God raised him from the dead, you will be saved. For it is with your heart that you believe and are justified, and it is with your mouth that you profess your faith and are saved.
Romans 10:9-10

The Sick, Weary & Discouraged

Do not be anxious about anything, but in everything by prayer and supplication with thanksgiving let your requests be made known to God. And the peace of God, which surpasses all understanding, will guard your hearts and your minds in Christ Jesus.
Philippians 4:6-7

The Oppressed & Enslaved

But as for me, I shall sing of Your strength; Yes, I shall joyfully sing of Your lovingkindness in the morning, For You have been my stronghold And a refuge in the day of my distress.
Psalm 59:16

I Y D W Y M, "J I L," A B I Y H T G R H F T D, Y W B S. F I I W Y H T Y B A A J, A I I W Y M T Y P Y F A A S. - Romans 10:9-10

D N B A A A, B I E B P A S W T L Y R B M K T G. A T P O G, W S A U, W G Y H A Y M I C J. - Philippians 4:6-7

B A F M, I S S O Y S; Y, I S J S O Y L I T M, F Y H B M S A A R I T D O M D. - Psalm 59:16

Wisdom

Everyone then who hears these words of mine and does them will be like a wise man who built his house on the rock.
Matthew 7:24

Daily Walk

But I say, walk by the Spirit, and you will not gratify the desires of the flesh.
Galatians 5:16

Gratitude & Joy

Instead, be filled with the Spirit, speaking to one another with psalms, hymns, and songs from the Spirit. Sing and make music from your heart to the Lord, always giving thanks to God the Father for everything, in the name of our Lord Jesus Christ.
Ephesians 5:18b-20

E T W H T W O M A D T W B L A W M W B H H O T R. - Matthew 7:24

B I S, W B T S, A Y W N G T D O T F. - Galatians 5:16

I, B F W T S, S T O A W P, H, A S F T S. S A M M F Y H T T L, A G T T G T F F E, I T N O O L J C. - Ephesians 5:18b-20

Adoration

Great and marvelous are your deeds, Lord God Almighty. Just and true are your ways, King of the nations. Who will not fear you, Lord, and bring glory to your name? For you alone are holy. All nations will come and worship before you, for your righteous acts have been revealed.
Revelation 15:3b-4

Confession

Those whom I love I rebuke and discipline. So be earnest and repent. Here I am! I stand at the door and knock. If anyone hears my voice and opens the door, I will come in and eat with that person, and they with me.
Revelation 3:19-20

Thanksgiving

Every good and perfect gift is from above, coming down from the Father of the heavenly lights, who does not change like shifting shadows.
James 1:17

G A M A Y D, L G A. J A T A Y W, K O T N. W W N F Y, L, A B G T Y N? F Y A A H. A N W C A W B Y, F Y R A H B R. - Revelation 15:3b-4

T W I L I R A D. S B E A R. H I A! I S A T D A K. I A H M V A O T D, I W C I A E W T P, A T W M. - Revelation 3:19-20

E G A P G I F A, C D F T F O T H L, W D N C L S S. - James 1:17

Children

Behold, children are a gift of the Lord. The fruit of the womb is a reward. Like arrows in the hand of a warrior, so are the children of one's youth.
Psalm 127:3-4

Marriages

Two are better than one, because they have a good reward for their labor. For if they fall, one will lift up his companion. But woe to him who is alone when he falls, for he has no one to help him up.
Ecclesiastes 4:9-10

Finances & Stewardship

Choose a good reputation over great riches; being held in high esteem is better than silver or gold. The rich and poor have this in common: The Lord made them both.
Proverbs 22:1-2

B, C A A G O T L. T F O T W I A R. L A I T H O A W, S A T C O O Y. - Psalm 127:3-4

T A B T O, B T H A G R F T L. F I T F, O W L U H C. B W T H W I A W H F, F H H N O T H H U. - Ecclesiastes 4:9-10

C A G R O G R; B H I H E I B T S O G. T R A P H T I C: T L M T B. - Proverbs 22:1-2

The Church

God is spirit, and those who worship him must worship in spirit and truth.
John 4:24

Nations & Leaders

The king's heart is a stream of water in the hand of the Lord; he turns it wherever he will.
Proverbs 21:1

Missionaries

Preach the word of God. Be prepared, whether the time is favorable or not. Patiently correct, rebuke, and encourage your people with good teaching.
2 Timothy 4:2

G I S, A T W W H M W I S A T. - John 4:24
T K H I A S O W I T H O T L; H T I W H W. - Proverbs 21:1
P T W O G. B P, W T T I F O N. P C, R, A E Y P W G T. - 2 Timothy 4:2

The Lost

And I will give them one heart, and a new spirit I will put within them. I will remove the heart of stone from their flesh and give them a heart of flesh, that they may walk in my statutes and keep my rules and obey them. And they shall be my people, and I will be their God.
Ezekiel 11:19-20

The Sick, Weary & Discouraged

Fear not, for I am with you; be not dismayed, for I am your God; I will strengthen you, I will help you, I will uphold you with my righteous right hand.
Isaiah 41:10

The Oppressed & Enslaved

The Spirit of the Lord is upon me, because he has anointed me to proclaim good news to the poor. He has sent me to proclaim liberty to the captives and recovering of sight to the blind, to set at liberty those who are oppressed.
Luke 4:18

AIWGTOH, AANSIWPWT. IWRTHOSFTFAGTAHOF, TTMWIMSAKMRAOT. ATSBMP, AIWBTG. - Ezekiel 11:19-20

FN, FIAWY; BND, FIAYG; IWSY, IWHY, IWUYWMRRH. - Isaiah 41:10

TSOTLIUM, BHHAMTPGNTTP. HHSMT PLTTCAROSTTB, TSALTWAO. - Luke 4:18

Wisdom

Don't be impressed with your own wisdom. Instead, fear the Lord and turn away from evil. Then you will have healing for your body and strength for your bones.
Proverbs 3:7-8

Daily Walk

Take delight in the Lord, and he will give you your heart's desires. Commit everything you do to the Lord. Trust him, and he will help you.
Psalm 7:4-5

Gratitude & Joy

I pray that God, the source of hope, will fill you completely with joy and peace because you trust in him. Then you will overflow with confident hope through the power of the Holy Spirit.
Romans 15:13

D B I W Y O W. I, F T L A T A F E. T Y W H H F Y B A S F Y B. - Proverbs 3:7-8

T D I T L, A H W G Y Y H D. C E Y D T T L. T H, A H W H Y. - Psalm 7:4-5

I P T G, T S O H, W F Y C W J A P B Y T I H. T Y W O W C H T T P O T H S. - Romans 15:13

Adoration

I will exalt you, my God and King, and praise your name forever and ever. I will praise you every day; yes, I will praise you forever. Great is the Lord! He is most worthy of praise! No one can measure his greatness.
Psalm 145:1-3

Confession

Have mercy on me, O God, because of your unfailing love. Because of your great compassion, blot out the stain of my sins. Wash me clean from my guilt. Purify me from my sin. For I recognize my rebellion; it haunts me day and night.
Psalm 51:1-3

Thanksgiving

Since we are receiving a Kingdom that is unshakable, let us be thankful and please God by worshiping him with holy fear and awe.
Hebrews 12:18

IWEY,MGAK,APYNFAE.IWPYED;Y,IWPYF.GITL! HIMWOP!NOCMHG. - Psalm 145:1-3

HMOM,OG,BOYUL,BOYGC,BOTSOMS.WMCFMG. PMFMS.FIRMR;IHMDAN. - Psalm 51:1-3

SWARAKTIU,LUBTAPGBWHWHFAA. - Hebrews 12:18

Children

....That their hearts may be encouraged, being knit together in love, to reach all the riches of full assurance of understanding and the knowledge of God's mystery, which is Christ.
Colossians 2:2

Marriages

Do not let any unwholesome talk come out of your mouths, but only what is helpful for building others up according to their needs, that it may benefit those who listen.
Ephesians 4:29

Finances & Stewardship

Whoever loves money never has enough; whoever loves wealth is never satisfied with their income. This too is meaningless.
Ecclesiastes 5:10

...T T H M B E, B K T I L, T R A T R O F A O U A T K O G M, W I C. - Colossians 2:2

D N L A U T C O O Y M, B O W I H F B O U A T T N, T I M B T W L. - Ephesians 4:29

W L M N H E; W L W I N S W T I. T T I M. - Ecclesiastes 5:10

The Church

A new commandment I give to you,
that you love one another: just as I have
loved you, you also are to love one another.
By this all people will know that you are
my disciples, if you have love
for one another.
John 13:34-35

Nations & Leaders

What joy for the nation whose God
is the Lord, whose people he
has chosen as his inheritance.
Psalm 33:12

Missionaries

But you should keep a clear mind in
every situation. Don't be afraid of suffering
for the Lord. Work at telling others the
Good News, and fully carry out the
ministry God has given you.
2 Timothy 4:5

A N C I G T O Y, T Y L O A: J A I H L Y, Y A A T L O A.
B T A P W K T Y A M D, I Y H L F O A. - John 13:34-35

W J F T N W G I T L, W P H H C A H I. - Psalm 33:12

B Y S K A C M I E S. D B A O S F T L. W A T O T G N, A F C O T M G H G Y. - 2 Timothy 4:5

The Lost

Gently instruct those who oppose the truth. Perhaps God will change those people's hearts, and they will learn the truth. Then they will come to their senses and escape from the devil's trap. For they have been held captive by him to do whatever he wants.
2 Timothy 2:25-26

The Sick, Weary & Discouraged

I have told you these things, so that in me you may have peace. In this world you will have trouble. But take heart! I have overcome the world.
John 16:33

The Oppressed & Enslaved

When I am afraid, I put my trust in you. In God, whose word I praise—in God I trust and am not afraid. What can mere mortals do to me?
Psalm 56:3-4

GITWOTT. PGWCTPH, ATWLTT. TTWCTTS AEFTDT. FTHBHCBHTDWHW. - 2 Timothy 2:25-26

IHTYTT, STIMYMHP. ITWYWHT. BTH! IHOTW. - John 16:33

WIAA, IPMTIY. IG, WWIP - IGITAANA. WCMMDTM? - Psalm 56:3-4

Wisdom

Be very careful, then, how you live—not as unwise but as wise, making the most of every opportunity, because the days are evil.
Ephesians 5:15-16

Daily Walk

Since, then, you have been raised with Christ, set your hearts on things above, where Christ is, seated at the right hand of God. Set your minds on things above, not on earthly things. For you died, and your life is now hidden with Christ in God.
Colossians 3:1-3

Gratitude & Joy

You make known to me the path of life; in your presence there is fullness of joy; at your right hand are pleasures forevermore.
Psalm 16:11

B V C, T, H Y L - N A U B A W, M T M O E O, B T D A E. - Ephesians 5:15-16

S, T, Y H B R W C, S Y H O T A, W C I, S A T R H O G. S Y M O T A, N O E T. F Y D, A Y L I N H W C I G. - Colossians 3:1-3

Y M K T M T P O L; I Y P T I F O J; A Y R H A P F. - Psalm 16:11

Adoration

Because your love is better than life, my lips will glorify you. I will praise you as long as I live, and in your name I will lift up my hands. I will be fully satisfied as with the richest of foods; with singing lips my mouth will praise you.
Psalm 63: 3-5

Confession

Whoever conceals their sins does not prosper, but the one who confesses and renounces them finds mercy.
Proverbs 28:13

Thanksgiving

Rejoice always, pray continually, give thanks in all circumstances; for this is God's will for you in Christ Jesus.
1 Thessalonians 5:16-18

B Y L I B T L, M L W G Y. I W P Y A L A I L, A I Y N I W L U M H. I W
B F S A W T R O F; W S L M M W P Y. - Psalm 63:3-5

W C T S D N P, B T O W C A R T F M. - Proverbs 28:13

R A, P C, G T I A C; F T I G W F Y I C J. - 1 Thessalonians 5:16-18

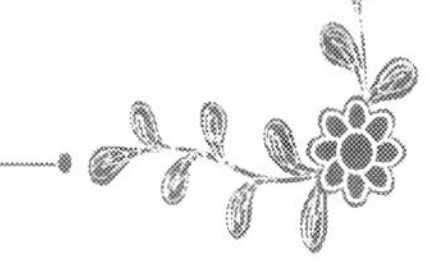

Children

May the Lord bless you and protect you. May the Lord smile on you and be gracious to you. May the Lord show you his favor and give you his peace.
Numbers 6:24-26

Marriages

May God, who gives this patience and encouragement, help you live in complete harmony with each other, as is fitting for followers of Christ Jesus. Then all of you can join together with one voice, giving praise and glory to God, the Father of our Lord Jesus Christ.
Romans 15:5-6

Finances & Stewardship

Keep your lives free from the love of money and be content with what you have, because God has said, "Never will I leave you; never will I forsake you."
Hebrews 13:5

M T L B Y A P Y. M T L S O Y A B G T Y. M T L S Y H F A G Y H P. - Numbers 6:24-26

M G, W G T P A E, H Y L I C H W E O, A I F F F O C J. T A O Y C J T W O V, G P A G T G, T F O O L J C. - Romans 15:5-6

K Y L F F T L O M A B C W W Y H, B G H S, "N W I L Y; N W I F Y." - Hebrews 13:5

The Church

If my people who are called by my name humble themselves, and pray and seek my face and turn from their wicked ways, then I will hear from heaven and will forgive their sin and heal their land.
2 Chronicles 7:14

Nations & Leaders

For our struggle is not against flesh and blood, but against the rulers, against the authorities, against the powers of this dark world and against the spiritual forces of evil in the heavenly realms.
Ephesians 6:12

Missionaries

Then he said to his disciples, "The harvest is plentiful but the workers are few. Ask the Lord of the harvest, therefore, to send out workers into his harvest field."
Matthew 9:27-28

I M P W A C B M N H T, A P A S M F A T F T W W, T I W H F H A W F T S A H T L. - 2 Chronicles 7:14

F O S I N A F A B, B A T R, A T A, A T P O T D W A A T S F O E I T H R. - Ephesians 6:12

T H S T H D, "T H I P B T W A F. A T L O T H, T, T S O W I H H F. - Matthew 9:27-28

The Lost

No one can come to me unless the Father who sent me draws them, and I will raise them up at the last day. It is written in the Prophets: 'They will all be taught by God.'
John 6:44-45

The Sick, Weary & Discouraged

The Lord gives strength to his people; the Lord blesses his people with peace.
Psalm 29:11

The Oppressed & Enslaved

The Lord is good, a strong refuge when trouble comes. He is close to those who trust in him. But he will sweep away his enemies in an overwhelming flood. He will pursue his foes into the darkness of night.
Nahum 1:7-8

N O C C T M U T F W S M D T, A I W R T U A T L D. I I W I T P: 'T W A B T B G.' - John 6:44-45

T L G S T H P; T L B H P W P. - Psalm 29:11

T L I G, A S R W T C. H I C T T W T I H. B H W S A H E I A O F. H W P H F I T D O N. - Nahum 1:7-8

Wisdom

If you are wise and understand God's ways, prove it by living an honorable life, doing good works with the humility that comes from wisdom.
James 3:13

Daily Walk

Beloved, let us love one another, for love is from God, and whoever loves has been born of God and knows God.
1 John 4:7

Gratitude & Joy

The commandments of the Lord are right, bringing joy to the heart. The commands of the Lord are clear, giving insight for living.
Psalm 19:8

I Y A W A U G W, P I B L A H L, D G W W T H T C F W. - James 3:13

B, L U L O A, F L I F G, A W L H B B O G A K G. - 1 John 4:7

T C O T L A R, B J T T H. T C O T L A C, G I F L. - Psalm 19:8

Adoration

I will extol you, my God and King, and bless your name forever and ever. Every day I will bless you and praise your name forever and ever. Great is the Lord, and greatly to be praised, and his greatness is unsearchable.
Psalm 145:1-3

Confession

Or do you show contempt for the riches of his kindness, forbearance and patience, not realizing that God's kindness is intended to lead you to repentance?
Romans 2:4

Thanksgiving

The Lord is my strength and my shield; my heart trusts in him, and he helps me. My heart leaps for joy, and with my song I praise him.
Psalm 28:7

I W E Y, M G A K, A B Y N F A E. E D I W B Y A P Y N F A E.
G I T L, A G T B P, A H G I U. - Psalm 145:1-3

O D Y S C F T R O H K, F A P, N R T G K I I T L Y T R? - Romans 2:4

T L I M S A M S; M H T I H, A H H M. M H L F J, A W M S I P H. - Psalm 28:7

Children

Do not conform to the pattern of this world, but be transformed by the renewing of your mind. Then you will be able to test and approve what God's will is—his good, pleasing and perfect will.
Romans 12:1-2

Marriages

Do nothing from selfish ambition or conceit, but in humility count others more significant than yourselves. Let each of you look not only to his own interests, but also to the interests of others.
Philippians 2:4-5

Finances & Stewardship

But godliness with contentment is great gain. For we brought nothing into the world, and we can take nothing out of it. But if we have food and clothing, we will be content with that.
1 Timothy 6:6-8

D N C T T P O T W, B B T B T R O Y M. T Y W B A T T A A W G W I - H G, P A P W. - Romans 12:1-2

D N F S A O C, B I H C O M S T Y. L E O Y L N O T H O I, B A T T I O O. - Philippians 2:4-5

B G W C I G G. F W B N I T W, A W C T N O O I. B I W H F A C, W W B C W T. 1 Timothy 6:6-8

The Church

May the God who gives endurance and encouragement give you the same attitude of mind toward each other that Christ Jesus had, so that with one mind and one voice you may glorify the God and Father of our Lord Jesus Christ.
Romans 15:5

Nations & Leaders

The fear of the Lord is the beginning of wisdom, and the knowledge of the Holy One is insight.
Proverbs 9:10

Missionaries

It's not important who does the planting, or who does the watering. What's important is that God makes the seed grow. The one who plants and the one who waters work together with the same purpose. And both will be rewarded for their own hard work.
1 Corinthians 3:7-8

MTGWGEAEGYTSAOMTEOTCJH, STWO MAOVYMGTGAFOOLJC. - Romans 15:5

TFOTLITBOW, ATKOTHOII. - Proverbs 9:10

INIWDTP, OWDTW. WIITGMTSG. TOWPATOWWWTW TSP. ABWBRFTOHW. - 1 Corinthians 3:7-8

The Lost

If you declare with your mouth, "Jesus is Lord," and believe in your heart that God raised him from the dead, you will be saved. For it is with your heart that you believe and are justified, and it is with your mouth that you profess your faith and are saved.
Romans 10:9-10

The Sick, Weary & Discouraged

Do not be anxious about anything, but in everything by prayer and supplication with thanksgiving let your requests be made known to God. And the peace of God, which surpasses all understanding, will guard your hearts and your minds in Christ Jesus.
Philippians 4:6-7

The Oppressed & Enslaved

But as for me, I shall sing of Your strength; Yes, I shall joyfully sing of Your lovingkindness in the morning, For You have been my stronghold And a refuge in the day of my distress.
Psalm 59:16

I Y D W Y M, "J I L," A B I Y H T G R H F T D, Y W B S. F I I W Y H T Y B A A J, A I I W Y M T Y P Y F A A S. - Romans 10:9-10

D N B A A A, B I E B P A S W T L Y R B M K T G. A T P O G, W S A U, W G Y H A Y M I C J. - Philippians 4:6-7

B A F M, I S S O Y S; Y, I S J S O Y L I T M, F Y H B M S A A R I T D O M D. - Psalm 59:16

Wisdom

Everyone then who hears these words of mine and does them will be like a wise man who built his house on the rock.
Matthew 7:24

Daily Walk

But I say, walk by the Spirit, and you will not gratify the desires of the flesh.
Galatians 5:16

Gratitude & Joy

Instead, be filled with the Spirit, speaking to one another with psalms, hymns, and songs from the Spirit. Sing and make music from your heart to the Lord, always giving thanks to God the Father for everything, in the name of our Lord Jesus Christ.
Ephesians 5:18b-20

E T W H T W O M A D T W B L A W M W B H H O T R. - Matthew 7:24

B I S, W B T S, A Y W N G T D O T F. - Galatians 5:16

I, B F W T S, S T O A W P, H, A S F T S. S A M M F Y H T T L, A G T T G T F F E, I T N O O L J C. - Ephesians 5:18b-20

Adoration

Great and marvelous are your deeds, Lord God Almighty. Just and true are your ways, King of the nations. Who will not fear you, Lord, and bring glory to your name? For you alone are holy. All nations will come and worship before you, for your righteous acts have been revealed.
Revelation 15:3b-4

Confession

Those whom I love I rebuke and discipline. So be earnest and repent. Here I am! I stand at the door and knock. If anyone hears my voice and opens the door, I will come in and eat with that person, and they with me.
Revelation 3:19-20

Thanksgiving

Every good and perfect gift is from above, coming down from the Father of the heavenly lights, who does not change like shifting shadows.
James 1:17

GAMAYD, LGA. JATAYW, KOTN. WWNFY, L, ABGT YN? FYAAH. ANWCAWBY, FYRAHBR. - Revelation 15:3b-4

TWILIRAD. SBEAR. HIA! ISATDAK. IAHMVAOTD, IWCIAEWTP, ATWM. - Revelation 3:19-20

EGAPGIFA, CDFTFOTHL, WDNCLSS. - James 1:17

Children

Behold, children are a gift of the Lord. The fruit of the womb is a reward. Like arrows in the hand of a warrior, so are the children of one's youth.
Psalm 127:3-4

Marriages

Two are better than one, because they have a good reward for their labor. For if they fall, one will lift up his companion. But woe to him who is alone when he falls, for he has no one to help him up.
Ecclesiastes 4:9-10

Finances & Stewardship

Choose a good reputation over great riches; being held in high esteem is better than silver or gold. The rich and poor have this in common: The Lord made them both.
Proverbs 22:1-2

B, C A A G O T L. T F O T W I A R. L A I T H O A W, S A T C O O Y. - Psalm 127:3-4

T A B T O, B T H A G R F T L. F I T F, O W L U H C. B W T H W I A W H F, F H H N O T H H U. - Ecclesiastes 4:9-10

C A G R O G R; B H I H E I B T S O G. T R A P H T I C: T L M T B. - Proverbs 22:1-2

The Church

God is spirit, and those who worship him must worship in spirit and truth.
John 4:24

Nations & Leaders

The king's heart is a stream of water in the hand of the Lord; he turns it wherever he will.
Proverbs 21:1

Missionaries

Preach the word of God. Be prepared, whether the time is favorable or not. Patiently correct, rebuke, and encourage your people with good teaching.
2 Timothy 4:2

G I S, A T W W H M W I S A T. - John 4:24

T K H I A S O W I T H O T L; H T I W H W. - Proverbs 21:1

P T W O G. B P, W T T I F O N. P C, R, A E Y P W G T. - 2 Timothy 4:2

The Lost

And I will give them one heart, and a new spirit I will put within them. I will remove the heart of stone from their flesh and give them a heart of flesh, that they may walk in my statutes and keep my rules and obey them. And they shall be my people, and I will be their God.
Ezekiel 11:19-20

The Sick, Weary & Discouraged

Fear not, for I am with you; be not dismayed, for I am your God; I will strengthen you, I will help you, I will uphold you with my righteous right hand.
Isaiah 41:10

The Oppressed & Enslaved

The Spirit of the Lord is upon me, because he has anointed me to proclaim good news to the poor. He has sent me to proclaim liberty to the captives and recovering of sight to the blind, to set at liberty those who are oppressed.
Luke 4:18

A I W G T O H, A A N S I W P W T. I W R T H O S F T F A G T A H O F, T T M W I M S A K M R A O T. A T S B M P, A I W B T G. - Ezekiel 11:19-20

F N, F I A W Y; B N D, F I A Y G; I W S Y, I W H Y, I W U Y W M R R H. - Isaiah 41:10

T S O T L I U M, B H H A M T P G N T T P. H H S M T P L T T C A R O S T T B, T S A L T W A O. - Luke 4:18

Wisdom

Don't be impressed with your own wisdom. Instead, fear the Lord and turn away from evil. Then you will have healing for your body and strength for your bones.
Proverbs 3:7-8

Daily Walk

Take delight in the Lord, and he will give you your heart's desires. Commit everything you do to the Lord. Trust him, and he will help you.
Psalm 7:4-5

Gratitude & Joy

I pray that God, the source of hope, will fill you completely with joy and peace because you trust in him. Then you will overflow with confident hope through the power of the Holy Spirit.
Romans 15:13

D B I W Y O W. I, F T L A T A F E. T Y W H H F Y B A S F Y B. - Proverbs 3:7-8

T D I T L, A H W G Y Y H D. C E Y D T T L. T H, A H W H Y. - Psalm 7:4-5

I P T G, T S O H, W F Y C W J A P B Y T I H. T Y W O W C H T T P O T H S. - Romans 15:13

Adoration

I will exalt you, my God and King, and praise your name forever and ever. I will praise you every day; yes, I will praise you forever. Great is the Lord! He is most worthy of praise! No one can measure his greatness.
Psalm 145:1-3

Confession

Have mercy on me, O God, because of your unfailing love. Because of your great compassion, blot out the stain of my sins. Wash me clean from my guilt. Purify me from my sin. For I recognize my rebellion; it haunts me day and night.
Psalm 51:1-3

Thanksgiving

Since we are receiving a Kingdom that is unshakable, let us be thankful and please God by worshiping him with holy fear and awe.
Hebrews 12:18

I W E Y, M G A K, A P Y N F A E. I W P Y E D; Y, I W P Y F. G I T L!
H I M W O P! N O C M H G. - Psalm 145:1-3

H M O M, O G, B O Y U L, B O Y G C, B O T S O M S. W M C F M G.
P M F M S. F I R M R; I H M D A N. - Psalm 51:1-3

S W A R A K T I U, L U B T A P G B W H W H F A A. - Hebrews 12:18

Children

....That their hearts may be encouraged, being knit together in love, to reach all the riches of full assurance of understanding and the knowledge of God's mystery, which is Christ.
Colossians 2:2

Marriages

Do not let any unwholesome talk come out of your mouths, but only what is helpful for building others up according to their needs, that it may benefit those who listen.
Ephesians 4:29

Finances & Stewardship

Whoever loves money never has enough; whoever loves wealth is never satisfied with their income. This too is meaningless.
Ecclesiastes 5:10

...T T H M B E, B K T I L, T R A T R O F A O U A T K O G M, W I C. - Colossians 2:2

D N L A U T C O O Y M, B O W I H F B O U A T T N, T I M B T W L. - Ephesians 4:29

W L M N H E; W L W I N S W T I. T T I M. - Ecclesiastes 5:10

The Church

A new commandment I give to you,
that you love one another: just as I have
loved you, you also are to love one another.
By this all people will know that you are
my disciples, if you have love
for one another.
John 13:34-35

Nations & Leaders

What joy for the nation whose God
is the Lord, whose people he
has chosen as his inheritance.
Psalm 33:12

Missionaries

But you should keep a clear mind in
every situation. Don't be afraid of suffering
for the Lord. Work at telling others the
Good News, and fully carry out the
ministry God has given you.
2 Timothy 4:5

A N C I G T O Y, T Y L O A: J A I H L Y, Y A A T L O A.
B T A P W K T Y A M D, I Y H L F O A. - John 13:34-35

W J F T N W G I T L, W P H H C A H I. - Psalm 33:12

B Y S K A C M I E S. D B A O S F T L. W A T O T G N, A F C O T M G H G Y. - 2 Timothy 4:5

The Lost

Gently instruct those who oppose the truth. Perhaps God will change those people's hearts, and they will learn the truth. Then they will come to their senses and escape from the devil's trap. For they have been held captive by him to do whatever he wants.
2 Timothy 2:25-26

The Sick, Weary & Discouraged

I have told you these things, so that in me you may have peace. In this world you will have trouble. But take heart! I have overcome the world.
John 16:33

The Oppressed & Enslaved

When I am afraid, I put my trust in you. In God, whose word I praise—in God I trust and am not afraid. What can mere mortals do to me?
Psalm 56:3-4

G I T W O T T. P G W C T P H, A T W L T T. T T W C T T S
A E F T D T. F T H B H C B H T D W H W. - 2 Timothy 2:25-26

I H T Y T T, S T I M Y M H P. I T W Y W H T. B T H! I H O T W. - John 16:33

W I A A, I P M T I Y. I G, W W I P - I G I T A A N A. W C M M D T M? - Psalm 56:3-4

Wisdom

Be very careful, then, how you live—
not as unwise but as wise, making the
most of every opportunity, because
the days are evil.
Ephesians 5:15-16

Daily Walk

Since, then, you have been raised with
Christ, set your hearts on things above,
where Christ is, seated at the right hand
of God. Set your minds on things above,
not on earthly things. For you
died, and your life is now
hidden with Christ in God.
Colossians 3:1-3

Gratitude & Joy

You make known to me the path of
life; in your presence there is
fullness of joy; at your right
hand are pleasures forevermore.
Psalm 16:11

BVC,T,HYL-NAUBAW,MTMOEO,BTDAE. - Ephesians 5:15-16

S,T,YHBRWC,SYHOTA,WCI,SATRHOG.SYMOTA,
NOET.FYD,AYLINHWCIG. - Colossians 3:1-3

YMKTMTPOL;IYPTIFOJ;AYRHAPF. - Psalm 16:11

Adoration

Because your love is better than life, my lips will glorify you. I will praise you as long as I live, and in your name I will lift up my hands. I will be fully satisfied as with the richest of foods; with singing lips my mouth will praise you.
Psalm 63: 3-5

Confession

Whoever conceals their sins does not prosper, but the one who confesses and renounces them finds mercy.
Proverbs 28:13

Thanksgiving

Rejoice always, pray continually, give thanks in all circumstances; for this is God's will for you in Christ Jesus.
1 Thessalonians 5:16-18

B Y L I B T L, M L W G Y. I W P Y A L A I L, A I Y N I W L U M H. I W B F S A W T R O F; W S L M M W P Y. - Psalm 63:3-5

W C T S D N P, B T O W C A R T F M. - Proverbs 28:13

R A, P C, G T I A C; F T I G W F Y I C J. - 1 Thessalonians 5:16-18

Children

May the Lord bless you and protect you. May the Lord smile on you and be gracious to you. May the Lord show you his favor and give you his peace.
Numbers 6:24-26

Marriages

May God, who gives this patience and encouragement, help you live in complete harmony with each other, as is fitting for followers of Christ Jesus. Then all of you can join together with one voice, giving praise and glory to God, the Father of our Lord Jesus Christ.
Romans 15:5-6

Finances & Stewardship

Keep your lives free from the love of money and be content with what you have, because God has said, "Never will I leave you; never will I forsake you."
Hebrews 13:5

M T L B Y A P Y. M T L S O Y A B G T Y. M T L S Y H F A G Y H P. - Numbers 6:24-26

M G, W G T P A E, H Y L I C H W E O, A I F F F O C J. T A O Y C J T W O V, G P A G T G, T F O O L J C. - Romans 15:5-6

K Y L F F T L O M A B C W W Y H, B G H S, "N W I L Y; N W I F Y." - Hebrews 13:5

The Church

If my people who are called by my name humble themselves, and pray and seek my face and turn from their wicked ways, then I will hear from heaven and will forgive their sin and heal their land.
2 Chronicles 7:14

Nations & Leaders

For our struggle is not against flesh and blood, but against the rulers, against the authorities, against the powers of this dark world and against the spiritual forces of evil in the heavenly realms.
Ephesians 6:12

Missionaries

Then he said to his disciples, "The harvest is plentiful but the workers are few. Ask the Lord of the harvest, therefore, to send out workers into his harvest field."
Matthew 9:27-28

I M P W A C B M N H T, A P A S M F A T F T W W, T I W H F H A W F T S A H T L. - 2 Chronicles 7:14

F O S I N A F A B, B A T R, A T A, A T P O T D W A A T S F O E I T H R. - Ephesians 6:12

T H S T H D, "T H I P B T W A F. A T L O T H, T, T S O W I H H F. - Matthew 9:27-28

The Lost

No one can come to me unless the Father who sent me draws them, and I will raise them up at the last day. It is written in the Prophets: 'They will all be taught by God.'
John 6:44-45

The Sick, Weary & Discouraged

The Lord gives strength to his people; the Lord blesses his people with peace.
Psalm 29:11

The Oppressed & Enslaved

The Lord is good, a strong refuge when trouble comes. He is close to those who trust in him. But he will sweep away his enemies in an overwhelming flood. He will pursue his foes into the darkness of night.
Nahum 1:7-8

N O C C T M U T F W S M D T, A I W R T U A T L D. I I W I T P: 'T W A B T B G.' - John 6:44-45

T L G S T H P; T L B H P W P. - Psalm 29:11

T L I G, A S R W T C. H I C T T W T I H. B H W S A H E I
A O F. H W P H F I T D O N. - Nahum 1:7-8

Wisdom

If you are wise and understand God's ways, prove it by living an honorable life, doing good works with the humility that comes from wisdom.
James 3:13

Daily Walk

Beloved, let us love one another, for love is from God, and whoever loves has been born of God and knows God.
1 John 4:7

Gratitude & Joy

The commandments of the Lord are right, bringing joy to the heart. The commands of the Lord are clear, giving insight for living.
Psalm 19:8

I Y A W A U G W, P I B L A H L, D G W W T H T C F W. - James 3:13

B, L U L O A, F L I F G, A W L H B B O G A K G. - 1 John 4:7

T C O T L A R, B J T T H. T C O T L A C, G I F L. - Psalm 19:8

Adoration

I will extol you, my God and King, and bless your name forever and ever. Every day I will bless you and praise your name forever and ever. Great is the Lord, and greatly to be praised, and his greatness is unsearchable.
Psalm 145:1-3

Confession

Or do you show contempt for the riches of his kindness, forbearance and patience, not realizing that God's kindness is intended to lead you to repentance?
Romans 2:4

Thanksgiving

The Lord is my strength and my shield; my heart trusts in him, and he helps me. My heart leaps for joy, and with my song I praise him.
Psalm 28:7

I W E Y, M G A K, A B Y N F A E. E D I W B Y A P Y N F A E.
G I T L, A G T B P, A H G I U. - Psalm 145:1-3

O D Y S C F T R O H K, F A P, N R T G K I I T L Y T R? - Romans 2:4

T L I M S A M S; M H T I H, A H H M. M H L F J, A W M S I P H. - Psalm 28:7

Children

Do not conform to the pattern of this world, but be transformed by the renewing of your mind. Then you will be able to test and approve what God's will is—his good, pleasing and perfect will.
Romans 12:1-2

Marriages

Do nothing from selfish ambition or conceit, but in humility count others more significant than yourselves. Let each of you look not only to his own interests, but also to the interests of others.
Philippians 2:4-5

Finances & Stewardship

But godliness with contentment is great gain. For we brought nothing into the world, and we can take nothing out of it. But if we have food and clothing, we will be content with that.
1 Timothy 6:6-8

D N C T T P O T W, B B T B T R O Y M. T Y W B A T T A A W G W I - H G, P A P W. - Romans 12:1-2

D N F S A O C, B I H C O M S T Y. L E O Y L N O T H O I, B A T T I O O. - Philippians 2:4-5

B G W C I G G. F W B N I T W, A W C T N O O I. B I
W H F A C, W W B C W T. 1 Timothy 6:6-8

The Church

May the God who gives endurance and encouragement give you the same attitude of mind toward each other that Christ Jesus had, so that with one mind and one voice you may glorify the God and Father of our Lord Jesus Christ.
Romans 15:5

Nations & Leaders

The fear of the Lord is the beginning of wisdom, and the knowledge of the Holy One is insight.
Proverbs 9:10

Missionaries

It's not important who does the planting, or who does the watering. What's important is that God makes the seed grow. The one who plants and the one who waters work together with the same purpose. And both will be rewarded for their own hard work.
1 Corinthians 3:7-8

MTGWGEAEGYTSAOMTEOTCJH, STWO MAOVYMGTGAFOOLJC. - Romans 15:5

TFOTLITBOW, ATKOTHOII. - Proverbs 9:10

INIWDTP, OWDTW. WIITGMTSG. TOWPATOWWWTW TSP. ABWBRFTOHW. - 1 Corinthians 3:7-8

The Lost

If you declare with your mouth, "Jesus is Lord," and believe in your heart that God raised him from the dead, you will be saved. For it is with your heart that you believe and are justified, and it is with your mouth that you profess your faith and are saved.
Romans 10:9-10

The Sick, Weary & Discouraged

Do not be anxious about anything, but in everything by prayer and supplication with thanksgiving let your requests be made known to God. And the peace of God, which surpasses all understanding, will guard your hearts and your minds in Christ Jesus.
Philippians 4:6-7

The Oppressed & Enslaved

But as for me, I shall sing of Your strength; Yes, I shall joyfully sing of Your lovingkindness in the morning, For You have been my stronghold And a refuge in the day of my distress.
Psalm 59:16

I Y D W Y M, "J I L," A B I Y H T G R H F T D, Y W B S. F I I W Y H T Y B A A J, A I I W Y M T Y P Y F A A S. - Romans 10:9-10

D N B A A A, B I E B P A S W T L Y R B M K T G. A T P O G, W S A U, W G Y H A Y M I C J. - Philippians 4:6-7

B A F M, I S S O Y S; Y, I S J S O Y L I T M, F Y H B M S A A R I T D O M D. - Psalm 59:16

Wisdom

Everyone then who hears these words of mine and does them will be like a wise man who built his house on the rock.
Matthew 7:24

Daily Walk

But I say, walk by the Spirit, and you will not gratify the desires of the flesh.
Galatians 5:16

Gratitude & Joy

Instead, be filled with the Spirit, speaking to one another with psalms, hymns, and songs from the Spirit. Sing and make music from your heart to the Lord, always giving thanks to God the Father for everything, in the name of our Lord Jesus Christ.
Ephesians 5:18b-20

E T W H T W O M A D T W B L A W M W B H H O T R. - Matthew 7:24

B I S, W B T S, A Y W N G T D O T F. - Galatians 5:16

I, B F W T S, S T O A W P, H, A S F T S. S A M M F Y H T T L, A G T T G T F F E, I T N O O L J C. - Ephesians 5:18b-20

Adoration

Great and marvelous are your deeds, Lord God Almighty. Just and true are your ways, King of the nations. Who will not fear you, Lord, and bring glory to your name? For you alone are holy. All nations will come and worship before you, for your righteous acts have been revealed.
Revelation 15:3b-4

Confession

Those whom I love I rebuke and discipline. So be earnest and repent. Here I am! I stand at the door and knock. If anyone hears my voice and opens the door, I will come in and eat with that person, and they with me.
Revelation 3:19-20

Thanksgiving

Every good and perfect gift is from above, coming down from the Father of the heavenly lights, who does not change like shifting shadows.
James 1:17

G A M A Y D, L G A. J A T A Y W, K O T N. W W N F Y, L, A B G T Y N? F Y A A H. A N W C A W B Y, F Y R A H B R. - Revelation 15:3b-4

T W I L I R A D. S B E A R. H I A! I S A T D A K. I A H M V A O T D, I W C I A E W T P, A T W M. - Revelation 3:19-20

E G A P G I F A, C D F T F O T H L, W D N C L S S. - James 1:17

Children

Behold, children are a gift of the Lord. The fruit of the womb is a reward. Like arrows in the hand of a warrior, so are the children of one's youth.
Psalm 127:3-4

Marriages

Two are better than one, because they have a good reward for their labor. For if they fall, one will lift up his companion. But woe to him who is alone when he falls, for he has no one to help him up.
Ecclesiastes 4:9-10

Finances & Stewardship

Choose a good reputation over great riches; being held in high esteem is better than silver or gold. The rich and poor have this in common: The Lord made them both.
Proverbs 22:1-2

B, C A A G O T L. T F O T W I A R. L A I T H O A W, S A T C O O Y. - Psalm 127:3-4

T A B T O, B T H A G R F T L. F I T F, O W L U H C. B W T H W I A W H F, F H H N O T H H U. - Ecclesiastes 4:9-10

C A G R O G R; B H I H E I B T S O G. T R A P H T I C: T L M T B. - Proverbs 22:1-2

The Church

God is spirit, and those who worship him must worship in spirit and truth.
John 4:24

Nations & Leaders

The king's heart is a stream of water in the hand of the Lord; he turns it wherever he will.
Proverbs 21:1

Missionaries

Preach the word of God. Be prepared, whether the time is favorable or not. Patiently correct, rebuke, and encourage your people with good teaching.
2 Timothy 4:2

G I S, A T W W H M W I S A T. - John 4:24

T K H I A S O W I T H O T L; H T I W H W. - Proverbs 21:1

P T W O G. B P, W T T I F O N. P C, R, A E Y P W G T. - 2 Timothy 4:2

The Lost

And I will give them one heart, and a new spirit I will put within them. I will remove the heart of stone from their flesh and give them a heart of flesh, that they may walk in my statutes and keep my rules and obey them. And they shall be my people, and I will be their God.
Ezekiel 11:19-20

The Sick, Weary & Discouraged

Fear not, for I am with you; be not dismayed, for I am your God; I will strengthen you, I will help you, I will uphold you with my righteous right hand.
Isaiah 41:10

The Oppressed & Enslaved

The Spirit of the Lord is upon me, because he has anointed me to proclaim good news to the poor. He has sent me to proclaim liberty to the captives and recovering of sight to the blind, to set at liberty those who are oppressed.
Luke 4:18

AIWGTOH, AANSIWPWT. IWRTHOSFTFAGTAHOF, TTMWIMSAKMRAOT. ATSBMP, AIWBTG. - Ezekiel 11:19-20

FN, FIAWY; BND, FIAYG; IWSY, IWHY, IWUYWMRRH. - Isaiah 41:10

TSOTLIUM, BHHAMTPGNTTP. HHSMT PLTTCAROSTTB, TSALTWAO. - Luke 4:18

Wisdom

Don't be impressed with your own wisdom. Instead, fear the Lord and turn away from evil. Then you will have healing for your body and strength for your bones.
Proverbs 3:7-8

Daily Walk

Take delight in the Lord, and he will give you your heart's desires. Commit everything you do to the Lord. Trust him, and he will help you.
Psalm 7:4-5

Gratitude & Joy

I pray that God, the source of hope, will fill you completely with joy and peace because you trust in him. Then you will overflow with confident hope through the power of the Holy Spirit.
Romans 15:13

D B I W Y O W. I, F T L A T A F E. T Y W H H F Y B A S F Y B. - Proverbs 3:7-8

T D I T L, A H W G Y Y H D. C E Y D T T L. T H, A H W H Y. - Psalm 7:4-5

I P T G, T S O H, W F Y C W J A P B Y T I H. T Y W O W C H T T P O T H S. - Romans 15:13

Adoration

I will exalt you, my God and King, and praise your name forever and ever. I will praise you every day; yes, I will praise you forever. Great is the Lord! He is most worthy of praise! No one can measure his greatness.
Psalm 145:1-3

Confession

Have mercy on me, O God, because of your unfailing love. Because of your great compassion, blot out the stain of my sins. Wash me clean from my guilt. Purify me from my sin. For I recognize my rebellion; it haunts me day and night.
Psalm 51:1-3

Thanksgiving

Since we are receiving a Kingdom that is unshakable, let us be thankful and please God by worshiping him with holy fear and awe.
Hebrews 12:18

I W E Y, M G A K, A P Y N F A E. I W P Y E D; Y, I W P Y F. G I T L! H I M W O P! N O C M H G. - Psalm 145:1-3

H M O M, O G, B O Y U L, B O Y G C, B O T S O M S. W M C F M G. P M F M S. F I R M R; I H M D A N. - Psalm 51:1-3

S W A R A K T I U, L U B T A P G B W H W H F A A. - Hebrews 12:18

Children

....That their hearts may be encouraged, being knit together in love, to reach all the riches of full assurance of understanding and the knowledge of God's mystery, which is Christ.
Colossians 2:2

Marriages

Do not let any unwholesome talk come out of your mouths, but only what is helpful for building others up according to their needs, that it may benefit those who listen.
Ephesians 4:29

Finances & Stewardship

Whoever loves money never has enough; whoever loves wealth is never satisfied with their income. This too is meaningless.
Ecclesiastes 5:10

...TTHMBE, BKTIL, TRATROFAOUATKOGM, WIC. - Colossians 2:2

DNLAUTCOOYM, BOWIHFBOUATTN, TIMBTWL. - Ephesians 4:29

WLMNHE; WLWINSWTI. TTIM. - Ecclesiastes 5:10

The Church

A new commandment I give to you,
that you love one another: just as I have
loved you, you also are to love one another.
By this all people will know that you are
my disciples, if you have love
for one another.
John 13:34-35

Nations & Leaders

What joy for the nation whose God
is the Lord, whose people he
has chosen as his inheritance.
Psalm 33:12

Missionaries

But you should keep a clear mind in
every situation. Don't be afraid of suffering
for the Lord. Work at telling others the
Good News, and fully carry out the
ministry God has given you.
2 Timothy 4:5

A N C I G T O Y, T Y L O A: J A I H L Y, Y A A T L O A.
B T A P W K T Y A M D, I Y H L F O A. - John 13:34-35

W J F T N W G I T L, W P H H C A H I. - Psalm 33:12

B Y S K A C M I E S. D B A O S F T L. W A T O T G N, A F C O T M G H G Y. - 2 Timothy 4:5

The Lost

Gently instruct those who oppose the truth. Perhaps God will change those people's hearts, and they will learn the truth. Then they will come to their senses and escape from the devil's trap. For they have been held captive by him to do whatever he wants.
2 Timothy 2:25-26

The Sick, Weary & Discouraged

I have told you these things, so that in me you may have peace. In this world you will have trouble. But take heart! I have overcome the world.
John 16:33

The Oppressed & Enslaved

When I am afraid, I put my trust in you. In God, whose word I praise—in God I trust and am not afraid. What can mere mortals do to me?
Psalm 56:3-4

GITWOTT. PGWCTPH, ATWLTT. TTWCTTS AEFTDT. FTHBHCBHTDWHW. - 2 Timothy 2:25-26

IHTYTT, STIMYMHP. ITWYWHT. BTH! IHOTW. - John 16:33

WIAA, IPMTIY. IG, WWIP - IGITAANA. WCMMDTM? - Psalm 56:3-4

Wisdom

Be very careful, then, how you live—
not as unwise but as wise, making the
most of every opportunity, because
the days are evil.
Ephesians 5:15-16

Daily Walk

Since, then, you have been raised with
Christ, set your hearts on things above,
where Christ is, seated at the right hand
of God. Set your minds on things above,
not on earthly things. For you
died, and your life is now
hidden with Christ in God.
Colossians 3:1-3

Gratitude & Joy

You make known to me the path of
life; in your presence there is
fullness of joy; at your right
hand are pleasures forevermore.
Psalm 16:11

BVC,T,HYL-NAUBAW,MTMOEO,BTDAE. - Ephesians 5:15-16

S,T,YHBRWC,SYHOTA,WCI,SATRHOG.SYMOTA,
NOET.FYD,AYLINHWCIG. - Colossians 3:1-3

YMKTMTPOL;IYPTIFOJ;AYRHAPF. - Psalm 16:11

Adoration

Because your love is better than life, my lips will glorify you. I will praise you as long as I live, and in your name I will lift up my hands. I will be fully satisfied as with the richest of foods; with singing lips my mouth will praise you.
Psalm 63: 3-5

Confession

Whoever conceals their sins does not prosper, but the one who confesses and renounces them finds mercy.
Proverbs 28:13

Thanksgiving

Rejoice always, pray continually, give thanks in all circumstances; for this is God's will for you in Christ Jesus.
1 Thessalonians 5:16-18

B Y L I B T L, M L W G Y. I W P Y A L A I L, A I Y N I W L U M H. I W B F S A W T R O F; W S L M M W P Y. - Psalm 63:3-5

W C T S D N P, B T O W C A R T F M. - Proverbs 28:13

R A, P C, G T I A C; F T I G W F Y I C J. - 1 Thessalonians 5:16-18

Children

May the Lord bless you and protect you. May the Lord smile on you and be gracious to you. May the Lord show you his favor and give you his peace.
Numbers 6:24-26

Marriages

May God, who gives this patience and encouragement, help you live in complete harmony with each other, as is fitting for followers of Christ Jesus. Then all of you can join together with one voice, giving praise and glory to God, the Father of our Lord Jesus Christ.
Romans 15:5-6

Finances & Stewardship

Keep your lives free from the love of money and be content with what you have, because God has said, "Never will I leave you; never will I forsake you."
Hebrews 13:5

MTLBYAPY. MTLSOYABGTY. MTLSYHFAGYHP. - Numbers 6:24-26

MG, WGTPAE, HYLICHWEO, AIFFFOCJ. TAOYCJTW OV, GPAGTG, TFOOLJC. - Romans 15:5-6

KYLFFTLOMABCWWYH, BGHS, "NWILY; NWIFY." - Hebrews 13:5

The Church

If my people who are called by my name
humble themselves, and pray and seek
my face and turn from their wicked ways,
then I will hear from heaven and will
forgive their sin and heal their land.
2 Chronicles 7:14

Nations & Leaders

For our struggle is not against flesh and
blood, but against the rulers, against
the authorities, against the powers of
this dark world and against the
spiritual forces of evil in the
heavenly realms.
Ephesians 6:12

Missionaries

Then he said to his disciples, "The
harvest is plentiful but the workers are
few. Ask the Lord of the harvest,
therefore, to send out workers
into his harvest field."
Matthew 9:27-28

I M P W A C B M N H T, A P A S M F A T F T W W, T I W H F H A W F T S A H T L. - 2 Chronicles 7:14

F O S I N A F A B, B A T R, A T A, A T P O T D W A A T S F O E I T H R. - Ephesians 6:12

T H S T H D, "T H I P B T W A F. A T L O T H, T, T S O W I H H F. - Matthew 9:27-28

The Lost

No one can come to me unless the Father who sent me draws them, and I will raise them up at the last day. It is written in the Prophets: 'They will all be taught by God.'
John 6:44-45

The Sick, Weary & Discouraged

The Lord gives strength to his people; the Lord blesses his people with peace.
Psalm 29:11

The Oppressed & Enslaved

The Lord is good, a strong refuge when trouble comes. He is close to those who trust in him. But he will sweep away his enemies in an overwhelming flood. He will pursue his foes into the darkness of night.
Nahum 1:7-8

N O C C T M U T F W S M D T, A I W R T U A T L D. I I W I T P: 'T W A B T B G.' - John 6:44-45

T L G S T H P; T L B H P W P. - Psalm 29:11

T L I G, A S R W T C. H I C T T W T I H. B H W S A H E I A O F. H W P H F I T D O N. - Nahum 1:7-8

Wisdom

If you are wise and understand God's ways, prove it by living an honorable life, doing good works with the humility that comes from wisdom.
James 3:13

Daily Walk

Beloved, let us love one another, for love is from God, and whoever loves has been born of God and knows God.
1 John 4:7

Gratitude & Joy

The commandments of the Lord are right, bringing joy to the heart. The commands of the Lord are clear, giving insight for living.
Psalm 19:8

I Y A W A U G W, P I B L A H L, D G W W T H T C F W. - James 3:13

B, L U L O A, F L I F G, A W L H B B O G A K G. - 1 John 4:7

T C O T L A R, B J T T H. T C O T L A C, G I F L. - Psalm 19:8

Adoration

I will extol you, my God and King, and bless your name forever and ever. Every day I will bless you and praise your name forever and ever. Great is the Lord, and greatly to be praised, and his greatness is unsearchable.
Psalm 145:1-3

Confession

Or do you show contempt for the riches of his kindness, forbearance and patience, not realizing that God's kindness is intended to lead you to repentance?
Romans 2:4

Thanksgiving

The Lord is my strength and my shield; my heart trusts in him, and he helps me. My heart leaps for joy, and with my song I praise him.
Psalm 28:7

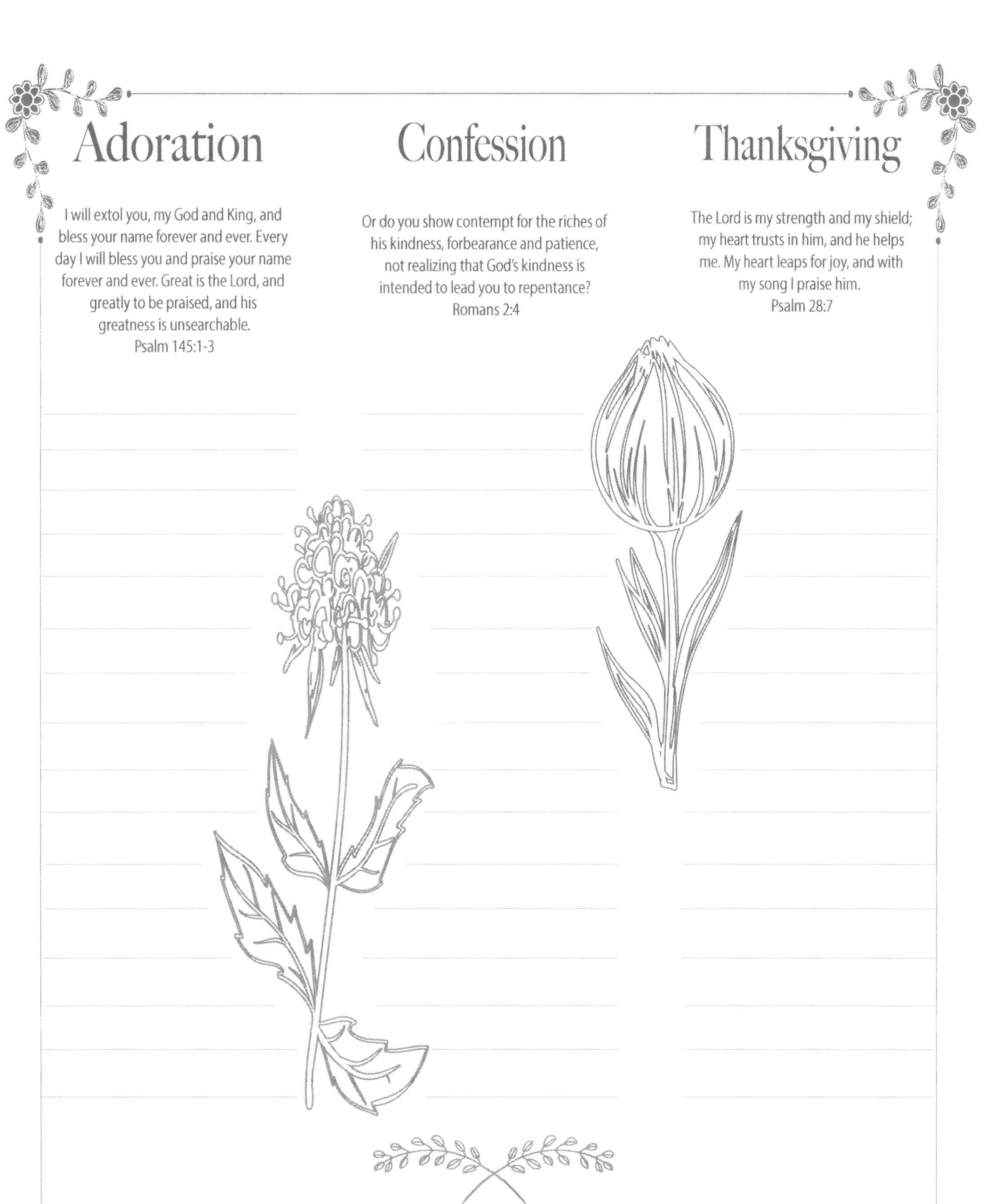

I W E Y, M G A K, A B Y N F A E. E D I W B Y A P Y N F A E. G I T L, A G T B P, A H G I U. - Psalm 145:1-3

O D Y S C F T R O H K, F A P, N R T G K I I T L Y T R? - Romans 2:4

T L I M S A M S; M H T I H, A H H M. M H L F J, A W M S I P H. - Psalm 28:7

Children

Do not conform to the pattern of this world, but be transformed by the renewing of your mind. Then you will be able to test and approve what God's will is—his good, pleasing and perfect will.
Romans 12:1-2

Marriages

Do nothing from selfish ambition or conceit, but in humility count others more significant than yourselves. Let each of you look not only to his own interests, but also to the interests of others.
Philippians 2:4-5

Finances & Stewardship

But godliness with contentment is great gain. For we brought nothing into the world, and we can take nothing out of it. But if we have food and clothing, we will be content with that.
1 Timothy 6:6-8

D N C T T P O T W, B B T B T R O Y M. T Y W B A T T A A W G W I - H G, P A P W. - Romans 12:1-2

D N F S A O C, B I H C O M S T Y. L E O Y L N O T H O I, B A T T I O O. - Philippians 2:4-5

B G W C I G G. F W B N I T W, A W C T N O O I. B I
W H F A C, W W B C W T. 1 Timothy 6:6-8

The Church

May the God who gives endurance and encouragement give you the same attitude of mind toward each other that Christ Jesus had, so that with one mind and one voice you may glorify the God and Father of our Lord Jesus Christ.
Romans 15:5

Nations & Leaders

The fear of the Lord is the beginning of wisdom, and the knowledge of the Holy One is insight.
Proverbs 9:10

Missionaries

It's not important who does the planting, or who does the watering. What's important is that God makes the seed grow. The one who plants and the one who waters work together with the same purpose. And both will be rewarded for their own hard work.
1 Corinthians 3:7-8

M T G W G E A E G Y T S A O M T E O T C J H, S T W O M A O V Y M G T G A F O O L J C. - Romans 15:5

T F O T L I T B O W, A T K O T H O I I. - Proverbs 9:10

I N I W D T P, O W D T W. W I I T G M T S G. T O W P A T O W W W T W T S P. A B W B R F T O H W. - 1 Corinthians 3:7-8

The Lost

If you declare with your mouth, "Jesus is Lord," and believe in your heart that God raised him from the dead, you will be saved. For it is with your heart that you believe and are justified, and it is with your mouth that you profess your faith and are saved.
Romans 10:9-10

The Sick, Weary & Discouraged

Do not be anxious about anything, but in everything by prayer and supplication with thanksgiving let your requests be made known to God. And the peace of God, which surpasses all understanding, will guard your hearts and your minds in Christ Jesus.
Philippians 4:6-7

The Oppressed & Enslaved

But as for me, I shall sing of Your strength; Yes, I shall joyfully sing of Your lovingkindness in the morning, For You have been my stronghold And a refuge in the day of my distress.
Psalm 59:16

IYDWYM,"JIL,"ABIYHTGRHFTD,YWBS.FIIWYHT YBAAJ,AIIWYMTYPYFAAS. - Romans 10:9-10

DNBAAA,BIEBPASWTLYRBMKTG.ATPOG, WSAU,WGYHAYMICJ. - Philippians 4:6-7

BAFM,ISSOYS;Y,ISJSOYLITM,FYHBMSAARITDOMD. - Psalm 59:16

Wisdom

Everyone then who hears these
words of mine and does them will
be like a wise man who built
his house on the rock.
Matthew 7:24

Daily Walk

But I say, walk by the Spirit,
and you will not gratify the
desires of the flesh.
Galatians 5:16

Gratitude & Joy

Instead, be filled with the Spirit,
speaking to one another with psalms,
hymns, and songs from the Spirit.
Sing and make music from your heart
to the Lord, always giving thanks to
God the Father for everything, in
the name of our Lord Jesus Christ.
Ephesians 5:18b-20

E T W H T W O M A D T W B L A W M W B H H O T R. - Matthew 7:24

B I S, W B T S, A Y W N G T D O T F. - Galatians 5:16

I, B F W T S, S T O A W P, H, A S F T S. S A M M F Y H T T L,
A G T T G T F F E, I T N O O L J C. - Ephesians 5:18b-20